THE GREAT RIFT

Africa Surgery Aids Aid

Michael and Elspeth King

ARCO BOOKS

THE GREAT RIFT

Africa Surgery Aids Aid

This book is copyright to the authors and all rights are reserved.

Artwork by Michael King

The authors regret any errors that may have been included. The opinions expressed are their own.

Published 2000 by ARCO BOOKS, P.O. Box 32, Cambridge
Printed by Victoire Press, Cambridge
ISBN 0-9539290-0-0

Michael King O.B.E. F.R.C.S. educated at St.John's College Cambridge and Guy's Hospital, Fellow of the Royal College of Surgeons of England 1966. He worked in Malaysia 1967-70, Swaziland 1970-73, and as Chief Government Surgeon in Malawi 1976-94. He has published several papers on surgery in international journals. Malawi Silver Jubilee Medal 1989, O.B.E. for services to surgery in developing countries, 1997.

Elspeth King Ph.D, his wife, educated at Cheltenham Ladies' College and London University. Ph.D. for research at the National Hospital for Nervous Diseases, London 1965. Lecturer in University of Malawi at the Polytechnic, Blantyre, 1980-94.

Contents

Introduction		1
Map		2
1. A Home in Africa	Hippo fracture; colonial house; school; visitors; family music; surgical interruptions; vervet monkeys; servants; malaria; witchcraft.	3
2. The Q.E.	Daily routine; rich and poor disease; cancer; clinical officers; heart stab; ectopic pregnancies; inappropriate technology and training; polio; very general surgeon. (M.K)	12
3. The Poor	Overpopulation; worsening poverty; fearful student reports; food aid; gangrene death; family planning; malnutrition; river trips; villages; aid policies.	21
4. The AIDS Epidemic	First cases; Kaposi's Sarcoma; denial; shingles; human rights; workshops; personal worries; let the dead bury their dead.	31
5. A Century of Surgery	Past and present; chest injuries; anaesthesia; amputations; tracheostomy; equipment; local doctors. (M.K)	41
6. Lake of Stars	Fishing; sailing; lake flies; development; student reports; declining catches; Jumbe; canoeing and camping; 'Ilala'.	49
7. Family Planning	Swaziland, Vatican, Donor and Malawian views; abortion; slow start; culture.	59
8. Sanjika Palace	President and Official Hostess; dictatorship; State banquets; Silver Jubilee Celebrations; Mrs. Thatcher; Mulanje Mountain.	67
9. The Grim AIDS Reaper	Disease patterns; deaths in high places; orphans; personal tales; witchcraft; surgical patients; 'non-discrimination'.	76

iv Contents

10. Dreams and Demons Tribal traditions; Nyau secret societies; fading 85
of Donor dreams; Polytechnic orchestra;
British Aid; Mission honesty; Mozambiquan
refugees; frontier night drive.

11. Polygamy in Africa Romantic and tribal emotion; sustained by 95
donor aid; marriage and land customs;
student views; malnutrition; AIDS;
institutionalized promiscuity.

12. Land of Fire Deforestation; mountain walks; student 102
views; trees to fire bricks; streams dry up;
conservation fails.

13. University Teaching Political intimidation of students and staff; 110
string Orchestra; secret meetings; publish and
perish; torture and death; prison conditions.

14. The Blantyre Riots Growing resentment; Catholic Bishops' Lenten 122
Letter; rioting mobs; gunshot casualties; BBC
reports; multiparty elections.

15. District Hospital Surgery Lakeside home; bewitchment; Rotary, worms; 129
tumours; ruptured spleen; bilharzia; witch
doctor; blocked by baobab seeds; brain clot;
staff resilience.   (M.K)

16. Sunrise and Sunset Termites; Christmas music; monkey troupe; 138
garden wildlife; lightning strike; river trip;
Berlin Orchestra; AIDS; Rabies; Sleeping
Sickness.

17. Health for All Comfortable words; community health; per 148
diems; medical costs; abortion; population
policy, conditional aid?   (M.K)

18. Amendment Can we make amends? 155

Appendices 157

Bibliography 158

Introduction

Malawi lies across the southern end of the Great Rift Valley of Africa. It is a small country of exhilarating beauty, with wild mountains, cascading streams, and the sparkling waters of Lake Malawi.

We have lived and worked there for twenty five years, Elspeth as a university lecturer and Michael as a surgeon. In this period the harsh rule of an absolute dictator gave way to a semblance of democracy - dangerous and dramatic times in which University students gave us insight into the social and cultural problems of their own people.

Today there is increasing poverty and declining health for most of the population. AIDS impacts on every family, and is often a hidden factor in already advanced surgical diseases.

Aid policies have largely failed to improve the situation and to some extent have made it worse. There is a Great Rift, or gap of understanding, between the rich nations and the poor villagers of Africa. With populations that are doubling every twenty years, the land and infrastructures are deteriorating. Perhaps the poor should be allowed the dignity of taking more responsibility for their own problems.

We have been privileged to live among the warm hearted people in a lovely but impoverished country. Every day has brought some new aspect, some uplift, some cause for reflection. But time is running out for the poor.

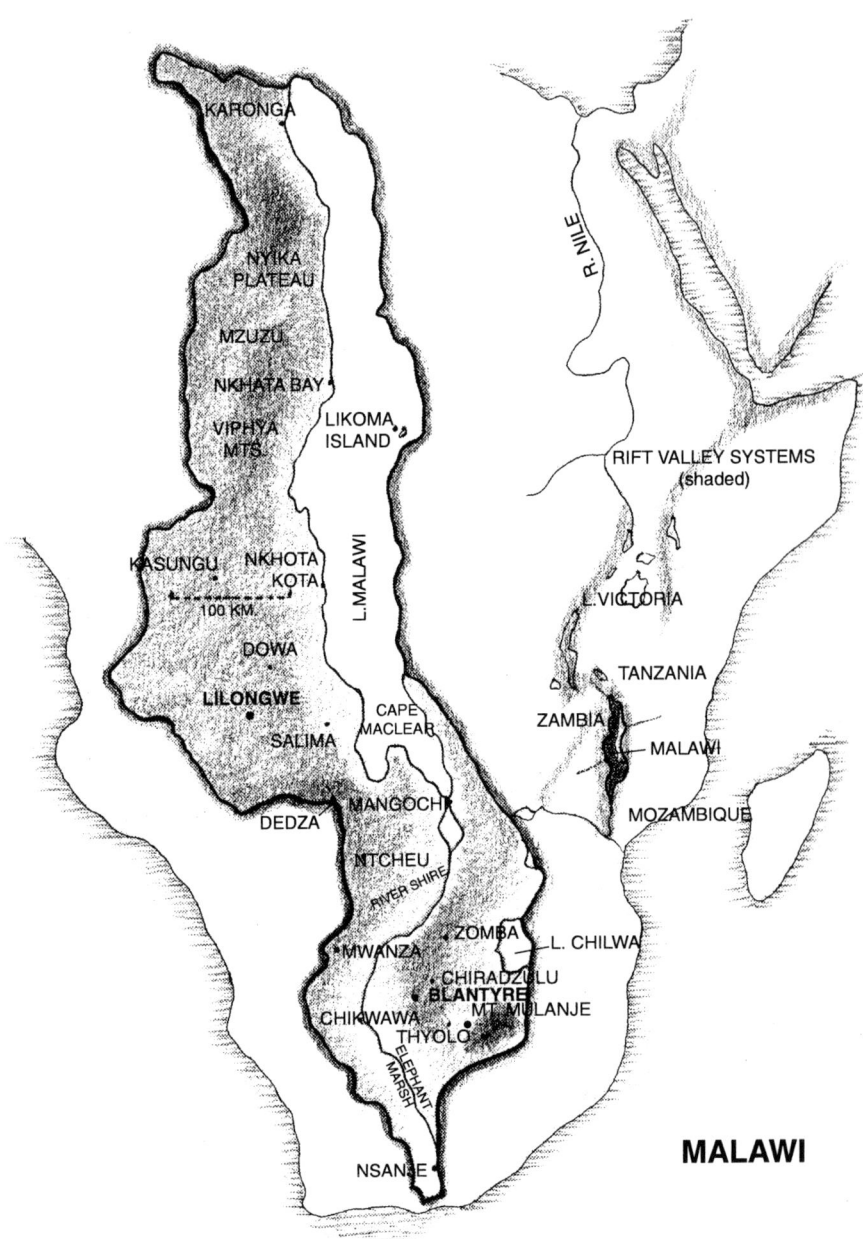

Chapter 1   A Home in Africa

First there was a heavy pounding of the ground, then the enraged hippopotamus burst out of the maize field into the moonlight, and literally ran over him before plunging down the bank into the river. The farmer had been shouting and banging saucepans with his fellow villagers to scare these huge animals from their fields. Hippos can weigh over a ton and he was lucky to escape with his life, without internal injuries.

When this man reached hospital, Michael put steel rods into both his broken thigh bones. Now, a year later, the patient had walked unaided into Chikwawa hospital beside the great Shire River, clad in bright yellow overalls. Michael had just returned up the escarpment road from the heat of the Great Rift Valley up to the cool of our home at Blantyre in the Shire Highlands, and he was telling me about his day. We had already lived there for three years.

It was in 1976 that we first reached Malawi at the zenith of the long, dry season. Under blue skies the land was yellow and brown and bush fires were burning on hazy, mauve hills. At noon, villagers were resting in the shade of their little mud and grass-thatched homes after hoeing the dessicated soil. Every inch of land here was cultivated, the gardens ready for planting extended up to the rocky summit of each hill. The parched land seemed to be crying out for rain, and heat radiated from the bare soil at midday. Only swaying banana groves and huge mango trees offered green relief and cooling shade.

Our destination was the garden city of Blantyre named after David Livingstone's birthplace in Scotland, and romantically founded when the pioneer Scots missionaries pitched their tents at the foot of Ndirande Mountain a century before. An old colonial house in Blantyre was allocated to us, close to Queen Victoria's Diamond Jubilee park, and recently vacated by the Vice President of Malawi, who had just been arrested; he was soon to be tried in a traditional court of chiefs for treason, and then hanged. I went to see the house with our daughters, to find the wife and his whole family sadly piling all their possessions on a lorry to return to their village. Under the dark clouds of the summer storms and with an overgrown garden, the place seemed full of gloom and doom that day.

British administrators had built this mansion with locally fired bricks before 1925, comprising six huge rooms and another seven small ones, together with a courtyard, many out-houses and a long colonnaded shady verandah for the hot season. However, after pruning the surrounding bushes and scything the grass, the house began to delight us. The vast semicircular front lawn must have been levelled for colonial garden parties in the twenties, and I could envisage the hats and dresses floating around in those distant days of elegance.

Cotton is a major crop in Malawi, so I used local material to furnish each room in a different colour, with hues of pinks, blues, mauves, and yellows. Our drawing room was enormous and here we made our quiet family haven. As there were no lampshades on sale, Michael cut some reeds and thorn branches in the bush and made hexagonal shapes covered with unbleached muslin. They became a resting place for the moths flying in from the scented blooms of our Queen of the Night bush outside the window.

We hung his sketches of Asia and Africa on the walls, and the room was transformed by the crimson carpets we had brought in Persia. With our piano, the spinet Michael had made in Britain, and our violins, viola, and cello, we could play music. This was our loved family home, always a source of enjoyment and interest.

In the tropics, natural invasions into a house are to be expected. As the summer rains flooded our lawns, moisture would seep up through cracks caused by spreading tree roots under our cement bedroom floor, soaking the mats. These crevices were also inhabited by other creatures – one night Michael put a copy of Darwin's 'Origin of Species' down beside our bed, and next morning he found it devoured by termites, which had come up during the night.

Then after the sunset, in the darkness, fireflies sparkled around our huge bedroom with staccato points of light. Michael was often called to do emergency operations at night, but I did not feel insecure. These typical nocturnal interruptions were recorded in my diary –

"Last night he was busy for three hours with a patient bleeding with liver cancer."

"He had to get up to operate on a patient from Chikwawa with an axe stuck a few inches into his head."

Michael had come to work as a surgeon supported by British government aid at the Queen Elizabeth Hospital, Blantyre. His first contract was for three years; but with our children we so enjoyed our life and work in Malawi that he stayed for two decades, as Chief Government Surgeon. He preferred the broader disciplines of the comprehensive surgery on younger patients needed in Africa. This contrasts with the narrow specialisms of surgery in the rich world, where the majority of surgical patients are elderly with degenerative disease. We had previously lived and worked in Malaysia and Swaziland.

We came to Blantyre because our daughters, Fiona and Sheenagh, could spend five happy years at St.Andrew's Secondary School, with children from fifty eight nations, and staffed by British and Rhodesian teachers. I was recruited to teach biology and violin lessons. The pupils were full of energy and motivation, a consequence perhaps of the prolific variety in the natural world around them in Central Africa.

For instance one boy often brought crocodile's eggs dug up from a sandy river bank, and another would arrive with snakes over his shoulder. Two German children, living at the Cabora Bassa dam on the Zambesi River, nearly lost a clarinet when the door of their tiny aeroplane flew open on their weekend journey home. Then a coloured boy told us tales about his great grandmother keeping slaves on an island in the middle of the Zambesi, and Asians described the machinations of arranged marriages. Some thought parents often made a good choice of spouse.

Mulanje Peaks

In the early years, our children were always busy with their school friends in many activities – discussing physics homework, running to catch Freddie our wandering donkey, cooking new recipes with local vegetables, feeding the lion cubs at the nearby little zoo, going to parties and dances, looking for snakes in the garden, or planning to climb Mulanje Mountain, the highest mountain in Central Africa. Their days were full.

Without television, we entertained ourselves. We had started playing as a family string quartet in Swaziland when our children were little. The African scene gave us a musical dimension we could not have experienced in modern Europe. We were not in competition, and played only for joy, surrounded by a landscape similar to the Europe of baroque and romantic composers.

After active days out of doors, and tea in the sunset, we would tune our instruments and perhaps play Mozart Serenades beside our window open to the enchanting moonlit tropical night, or Schubert's 'Trout' music in a land of mountains and cascading streams. Our dog, Sheik, would also try to participate, howling high notes at the top of his doggy serenading range, and looking sheepish when we led him to his mat by the back door. Often the family of Michael's Dutch surgical colleague, Jan Borgstein, played music with us, adding a violin, clarinet, trumpet, and accordion to our ensemble. With a more masculine orchestra – the Borgsteins had seven sons of whom six later qualified as doctors,- we enjoyed the firm notes of Bach and Haydn.

However, song birds have to fly from the nest, and when our daughters went off to University, our family string quartet suddenly vanished; it was replaced by visiting doctors, medical students, and German string players. In Africa one must be a jack of all trades, so I learned the cello too, taking an examination of the Royal Schools of Music.

As the examiner from Suffolk arrived for dinner, our cook Peter gave him a warm Malawian welcome at the kitchen door -"I am cooking you a good meal so that you will give madam good marks tomorrow!" We sat around our blazing log fire to hear his tales – he had just adjudicated in a tiny room in Ghana, where a booming local bass sang 'An English Country Garden' straight into his ear.

Relationships with servants are a rewarding aspect of life in Africa. In his ten years as our cook, Peter became our confidante, our protector, and our advisor about the increasingly insecure city around us, and he gave us insight into Malawian cultural problems. After we left Blantyre, his wife died, but he still writes to us, warmly recalling their years as part of our family.

Most nights we could rarely play a sonata without interruption from a phone call about medical problems – it is true a surgeon's service is never finished, for the needs of the sick were clamouring day and night. We would start a piece of music, wondering whether we could finish it before another grave problem intruded; my diary records a few of them, often coming whilst Michael was out at the hospital:

'Sunday March 1987 – On a very faint telephone line I hear the medical assistant speaking from Nsanje hospital, he is leaving at dawn tomorrow with two patients and hoping to reach Queen Elizabeth hospital in four hours. One boy had a head injury last week and now has low blood pressure, failing speech, and loss of memory. The other has a crocodile bite on his left arm with infection and a severe compound fracture."

"Thursday – The faint voice of the new British doctor at Rumphi hospital, seven hundred miles to the north, asks how to manage a ruptured spleen in a boy who has fallen from a mango tree."

"Friday – A visiting German doctor and his family have been gravely hurt in a road accident. This evening his distressed father phones from Europe. I try to comfort him – 'Please be re-assured, my husband is looking after them carefully, he has gone to them now. If you phone back in two hours he will be here to speak to you.'"

"Saturday – Michael had many problems this afternoon, including one patient with a gangrenous bowel and in surgical shock. The theatres were so busy with Caesarean sections that he could not get this urgent case to operation until 9 pm, even then he spent some time on the phone trying to persuade the maternity staff that more of their mothers might give birth to their babies normally in the ward!"

When Michael came home weary from the hospital, I often played gentle music to him from the FitzWilliam Virginal book on the spinet. But my musical efforts were sometimes beleaguered by creatures of nature. Once when our spinet was damp, with the wooden keys all swelling and sticking, I put a table lamp underneath it, and a sheet over the instrument to cloak the warmth and dry the wood. The following morning a musical mood having overtaken me, I hastily threw the sheet on the floor, and I was playing a favourite piece, 'Folia d'Espagne' by Alessandro Scarlatti, when a two foot long snake writhed out. Since that day, the graceful melodic structure of Scarlatti's musical composition always reminds me of this brilliant green snake's elegant writhing movement across our red Persian carpet.

The Snake and the Spinet

In Africa, entertaining visiting surgeons at home is a part of life. Over supper, we could tell visitors of Malawian problems, and the help that was needed, although many could not comprehend the problems of the high birthrate, because they did not see the consequences at first hand. Diplomats often visited us. One evening, at dusk, two London foreign office men arrived for a beer in our garden, just as a goshawk was eating a snake laid out on the branch of an overhanging tree. Over dinner we heard they had come to warn British staff, because several VSOs had returned from Malawi infected with HIV; Parliamentary questions were to be asked about the cost of this. But when they saw the forty or so greying, middle aged Britons at their Blantyre meeting, they did not think these cautions were necessary!

Another evening, several local doctors came to enjoy a dinner of pumpkin soup, chambo with lemons, tomatoes, and African sweet potatoes, followed by that queen of fruits, the mango. Our conversation first touched on falciparum malaria, then becoming drug-resistant. These parasites, transmitted by mosquito bites, multiply in the red blood cells. The speed with which malaria can overwhelm some expatriates with little immunity is alarming –

We heard of a young Scotsman who had arrived at a hospital feeling unwell in the morning, walked into a ward at noon, lost consciousness with cerebral malaria by teatime, and was brain dead at nightfall.

Then the interesting case of a New Zealand girl who died of 'algid' malaria after only three days in the ward and with no fever was described. Sudden death can lurk just around the corner in tropical Africa.

A visiting Addenbrooke's medical student had just seen a malnourished patient collapsing who had a haemoglobin of only 20%. In Europe, he would have been rushed for a blood transfusion. However the blood bank had run out of blood, so the medical assistants managed the case: the patient was fed with mashed bananas which are rich in sodium and potassium, pumpkin leaves as a source of iron, and an egg every day.

For many years Michael spent much time whilst at home 'on call to the hospital' with painting and sculpturing on our verandah. I wrote in a letter to our children: "October 1986 – Dad is now painting the panel of the Holy Family for the Anglican cathedral reredos, with Halley's Comet as the Star of Bethlehem. The donkey looks quite sweet, rather like Freddie when he used to look in at our verandah door as we were playing music. Last night, the moon was full and I went outside. Our garden was so lovely, all lit up, with moths fluttering around the Queen of the Night bushes. Yesterday a family of about fifteen monkeys came scampering over the lawn eating seeds from our long grass. I could see their debris – geranium shoots and bauhinia seed pods – in the evening moonlight. In the trees the bush babies were crying softly, and the gentle calls of the long eared African owls resounded with the singing of hundreds of frogs and crickets."

A troupe of about twenty wild vervet monkeys lived in our garden trees for years. They were always watching us with fraternity from the high trees, swinging in the branches, chasing each other at speed, noisily fighting over our guavas and loquats, raiding our vegetables, grooming each other in the morning sunshine, or rapidly copulating. In trying to outwit them, we failed and I grew to respect the intelligence of monkeys.

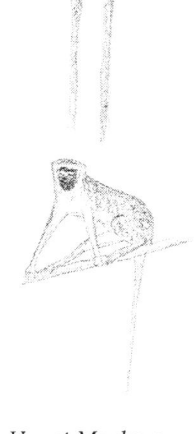

I wrote to Sheenagh "Today, as a Bach Orchestral Suite was resounding from our record player, sixteen monkeys came down again to sit on the lawn outside our drawing room window. One or two stayed up in the trees to keep a lookout, but a big male came nearest to our house, shepherding nine adults and five babies. They seem attracted by the thump of Bach and Handel, so someone could do a project on "Primate preference for baroque music"!

Vervet Monkeys

Fiona came home to do a research project on this troupe of monkeys for her Cambridge university tripos. Whilst wildlife experts in Europe believed in 'primate conservation', the poor Malawians crowding the land around the fringes of our garden were struggling every day to exterminate these monkeys to save their food and their lives. Fiona found that the gardens growing maize and beans suffered most from monkey invasion. It is easy to believe in animal protection when, miles away on the other side of the world, you can buy food at supermarkets. In Africa people have to keep dogs and fell trees to rid themselves of the monkeys that will wreck their crops.

After failing with a crossbow, catapult, and airgun to kill any monkeys, our servants once made a trap and caught three of them. It consisted of a bent flexible sapling and a string loop around some maize on the ground. When the monkey attempted to grab this bait, it triggered the sapling to spring upright, tightening the noose around his wrist, and the monkey was pulled up to hang screaming until he was despatched. The troupe soon learned to avoid this trap.

Stars are brilliantly visible in the equatorial night sky, and on many nights we enjoyed looking at the planets and constellations with binoculars. In March 1986 came Halley's Comet, and I wrote to our daughters: "On a cloudless night, we went along the Chikwawa road to a lonely spot looking down on the Great Rift Valley. The high, bare, deserted mountain peaks surrounded us. The Milky Way was brilliantly visible now at this equinox, from part of the Plough in the North down to the Southern Cross, and Saturn was a flaming orange. We saw the Comet above Soche mountain, with its luminous core and tail easily seen with the naked eye, looking like a tiny umbrella with a trailing veil. It differed from any other celestial body in the universe that night."

The mathematical predictability of this comet's eighty-six year orbit seemed a strange psychological invasion into the cultural atmosphere in Central Africa. In these tropical climes, nature is more powerful than mankind, and daily life is capricious, as storms, floods, dust, and insect invasions, may often thwart any human plans or events. Man cannot control his environment, and so he feels dependent on supernatural powers, on the spirits of his ancestors which determine his world. Our servants slowly opened our eyes to the witchcraft of Central Africa.

Our gardener, Wiseman, came from the Sena tribe in the Lower Shire Valley. I tried to help him by paying his fees for school each afternoon, and by buying items like tools to take home to his village. After two years with us, he was unexpectedly intimidated. Local political party members seized him in the street, taking him to be publicly humiliated and chastised by the Womens' League for swearing in the street. After I protested, I received telephone calls demanding my presence at the all powerful party head office – but I declined.

However when Wiseman went home to his village in 1985 worse trouble awaited him. His brother later told me how the other villagers were jealous of him. So witch doctors cast evil spells causing quarrels with his wife. He was then visited by her mother who shrieked that he was a rich town boy with too many clothes and goods. In anger he hurled a spear at her, killing her. He was taken to prison, incarcerated with hundreds of Malawians accused of murder and never brought to trial. Much later we heard that he had died in the crowded prison conditions. With his faithful service to us, Wiseman had surely earned all that we gave him. I can never forget such a tragedy.

Visiting us for tea beside a blazing fire one winter afternoon, a Catholic monk gave us more insight into these sad sorcery problems, when he commented: "Villages I have visited in Malawi have not changed in thirty years and there is still the same disease of envy. If one man makes more money, gets more educated, or gets a better job, then other people become jealous and he may be attacked, beaten, or bewitched. It takes a brave person to think that it is worth improving himself or progressing in this kind of witchcraft."

So, very gradually, from our own hearth and home, our eyes were opened to the real and tragic problems around us in Central Africa.

Chapter 2. The Q.E. MK

The Queen Elizabeth Hospital in Blantyre, or the 'QE', was opened by the Queen Mother in 1957. Built by the Federation of Rhodesia and Nyasaland Government, it replaced the Presbyterian African and Asian hospitals and the private European one in Blantyre. Well designed, with pavilioned wards interspersed with lawns and trees, patients can enjoy much of the day sitting outside in the sunshine. Behind is Mount Soche with rain forest at its summit as a magnificent backdrop. During the eighteen years that I trod its corridors many of the lawns were obliterated by new wards, and later, the teaching annexes of the medical school. The number of in-patients rose from the original four hundred and fifty to over a thousand.

A normal day would start with a quick round to discharge patients from the overcrowded wards, – most had forty-five beds but ninety patients. It was difficult to examine a patient on the floor under a bed! The operating list would occupy the rest of the morning. The average age of the patients was twenty years, compared with over sixty years in Britain. Some were there because many more surgical infections present in poor communities compared with rich countries, especially after the HIV-virus arrived. These problems included muscle abscesses containing

Ward Scene

several litres of pus, bone and joint infections, and typhoid perforations of the intestine. Many trauma patients were admitted, road traffic accidents heading the list of causes but with the occasional crocodile, snake, or hippo bite. Large malarial spleens rupture easily with even minor trauma and need removal.

Chronic surgical conditions are different from those of the rich world, where hospitals spend much of their time on degenerative conditions, hardening of the arteries, coronary disease, aneurysms, and arthritis of the hip and knees. All these conditions are rare in the poor world, probably due to differences in life style and diet, as are the differences in cancer incidence.

The colon in Malawians is large and long due to a high fibre vegetable diet, and does not develop cancer or diverticulitis easily, (as is so common in the rich world), but it is likely to twist and cause obstruction. Cancer of the oesophagus is much more common in Malawi than in the UK, probably related to diet. Bladder cancer is also depressingly common caused by the chronic irritation of Bilharzia, a water borne parasite which deposits its eggs in the bladder lining.

Breast cancer is less common, probably related to the protective effect of early pregnancies, but which factor in its turn is linked to the high incidence of cancer of the cervix in Africa. The most common cancer in the rich world occurs in the lung or bronchus, related to smoking. This is rare but increasing in Malawi, not surprising seeing that the main product and export commodity of the country is tobacco. The most common cancer in Malawi is probably Kaposi's sarcoma, related to HIV-infection; but this is a special case and is described later.

Many patients arrive late due to distances from hospitals and delay when using traditional medicines; however occasionally 'heroic' operations for both the patient and the surgeon would be done, such as removing whole stomachs or bladders. This would mean several patients with more simple routine operations were delayed – those with hernias, duodenal ulcers, enlarged prostates, needing skin grafts, or open reduction of fractures, and children with congenital deformities.

In 1976, when I arrived, there were the two original theatres used by the three or four surgeons and which were shared with the two obstetricians, (who later had their own unit). In the early nineties Malawi hosted a million Mozambiquan refugees, and as well as dealing with their daily routine surgical cases, landmine and battle casualties started coming in.

More theatres were needed so funds were obtained from the United Nations High Commission for Refugees (UNHCR) for two more theatres. I found it interesting designing and watching these theatres being built, taking ten months. They were simple, large and high, with windows that could open when the air conditioning failed, which it did often. There was a clear view of the operating table from the scrubbing up area, and of the sky and the treetops, important for everyone's composure.

In the afternoon there might be an out patient session. Ninety or so patients from all over Malawi would be examined, together with clinical officers or junior doctors. Dates would be given for operations, usually within a month. Throughout the day, the tannoy would be calling for medical staff to go urgently to the wards, but when this finally broke down, life was quieter, although it was a mixed blessing.

A final check on the post-operative patients or perhaps an emergency operation would be carried out before returning home. If 'on call', it was likely that I would have to return to review or operate on a patient that night. It could be tiring and worrying, especially with newly trained and unsure staff who needed guiding.

Over the years in spite of increasing problems, the QE has struggled to give a good free service to the community. It is not only the main referral hospital for a country of ten million people, but also a district hospital for a city of half a million. In the late 1970s, most of the doctors were Dutch and British on aid schemes, with some Malawians and Malawian Asians who had trained overseas. There was a good working relationship between the warm and generous Malawians and the more intense Europeans. In spite of scholarships abroad, few trained Malawians returned to their country, mainly because of poor salaries but also because of their distrust of the regime. There were many more Malawian doctors working in Manchester than in Malawi.

The College of Medicine opened in stages at the QE in 1991, with initial training in Britain. Today the full training is available in Malawi and produces over twenty doctors every year. It is disturbing for those from Africa who have trained in the rich world, or who go there for further training, to return to the almost totally different clinical problems, the lack of facilities, and poor salary, in their respective home countries. Many leave to work abroad, but an increasing number stay and face worsening clinical and administrative problems. Their training has been biased towards the 'community health' required by the donors.

In any case, for the everyday sick patient, Malawi will continue to rely not on doctors but on clinical officers and medical assistants. These are locally trained paramedics and most patients in district hospitals will be diagnosed, treated, and have operations performed by them. About five clinical officers and perhaps four medical assistants, with a doctor or senior clinical officer in charge, will run each district hospital. But the stark reality is that some of the forty or so district hospitals throughout Malawi have no doctor, whilst a few mission hospitals have more than one doctor. Even the three central hospitals, including the QE, rely heavily on these paramedics, who are often very good, skilled in surgery, and work the long hours required with aplomb and extraordinary stamina. They do not have the option of going abroad to work, and for the foreseeable future they are the only affordable way to deliver health care. The National Health Service in Britain could well draw some lessons here.

There were always difficulties; for two decades, apart from one short period, the QE had no radiologist and the hospital laboratory lacked any practising pathologist for half of that time. A good Malawian pathologist was taken out of the QE when he was recruited by World Health Organization to take charge of the AIDS control programme, at a much higher salary than the Malawi government could offer. Our biopsy specimens then had to be sent to St.Thomas' hospital in London, and if we were lucky we would hear a month later by telegram if a tumour was malignant or not. It could only get worse as patients lost the services of several other Malawian doctors and clinical officers who were periodically recruited by the UN agencies.

Every day the QE Hospital sees two thousand out-patients, well over a thousand in-patients, whilst over a month twelve hundred mothers give birth in the maternity department. The largest British hospitals, with many more staff, have five hundred deliveries a month. There are increasing shortages of drugs and surgical supplies, which makes the notion of cost sharing or patient charging essential; a free service can simply be no longer sustained, even though politically there is a reluctance to introduce fees. What has happened therefore is the growth of some mission and private hospitals serving the better off in the city. Increasingly the more affluent take out medical insurance schemes so they can fly to South Africa or Zimbabwe.

However emergencies continue to arrive in which at least initial treatment must be given without delay, such as an Indian who had been stabbed:

I saw him in casualty with blood gushing from a half inch wound in the chest. I remember there was so much blood everywhere that it was a wonder there was any more left to pump out. At operation, the spurting wound in the right chamber of the heart was closed with a few stitches and a tube put into the chest to allow the collapsed left lung to expand. The next day he was doing well but the Asian community wanted him to be transferred to South Africa. We arranged for a Medivac team with its intensive care small jet to fly up from Johannesburg. On the flight

Night Operation

there he had a cardiac arrest, but they were able to restart the heart. A few days later in Johannesburg an angiogram X-ray showed blood was being shunted through a hole between the right and left chambers of the heart, which threatened heart failure. So he was re-operated, the heart was opened, using a by-pass, and the hole was closed. He made a slow recovery and eventually returned to Malawi. It was a story with numerous turns but with a happy outcome.

The general surgeon in poor Africa would only carry out cardio-thoracic surgery in emergency situations such as these, apart from some simple proceedures. However, poorer countries have set up expensive units which are often inappropriate and drain funds which would be better used for simpler life saving surgery. For example, for every hernia operated on in East Africa, there are probably five times that number not treated. A strangulated or 'stuck' hernia patient not operated on will probably die, and any hernia is liable to become strangulated. Similarly there are many African mothers with obstructed labour who need Caesarian sections and never get them and their babies die. The mothers may die or they suffer permanent damage, especially to their bladders, due to prolonged pressure of the baby's head, resulting in continuous leakage of urine for the rest of their lives.

General surgery and gynaecology often overlap, perhaps most commonly in ectopic (in the wrong place) pregnancies. This is common in Africa and may be related to previous infections. The woman, in the early weeks of pregnancy, is seized with severe abdominal pain and collapses in shock as the pregnancy ruptures the uterine tube and causes internal bleeding. Urgent operation and blood transfusion is then needed. The loose blood in the abdomen is retransfused into the patient and the tube is removed, leaving the other one to allow further, and hopefully uterine, pregnancies. This operation is carried out regularly by the clinical officers.

Some extraordinary ectopic pregnancies are seen. A lady presented with a liver swelling thought to be a liver cancer – which is quite common in Africa. The admitting doctor examining her found the tumour gave him a kick! No normal delivery could be expected, and since the baby was about full term, an operation was planned. The patient, fearful of this, then ran off, only to return a few days later. Unfortunately by then no foetal movements were felt and no foetal heart heard. At operation, the dead foetus and placenta were completely enclosed by liver tissue, which had to be incised to release and remove the remains. In the beginning, the fertilized egg, instead of descending down the fallopian tube to implant in the uterus, had floated around the abdominal cavity and implanted in one of the folds of the liver. Liver tissue had grown round this early pregnancy, producing this unusual liver 'tumour' months later.

Another case presented as an abscess of the abdominal wall through which came pus and eventually pieces of foetal bone. Two years earlier the patient believed she was pregnant but never delivered. The foetus which was developing outside the womb, attached to the intestines, died and the soft tissue was absorbed. Unluckily infection settled around the remaining bones causing an abscess. In the rich world early investigations into abnormalities of pregnancy would have prevented such gross pathology.

The auhor showing the Life President Dr Banda a patient on his Christmas Day visit (from a photo)

Any doctor who has worked in the poor world where patients present late has a fund of similar stories. It is important that doctors in remote areas are able to do some surgery, and that surgeons have a broad general training. They will have to deal with obstructed labours, perforated bowels causing peritonitis, foreign bodies (seeds, coins) in every orifice, chest and abdominal abscesses needing drainage, burns, and fractured and damaged limbs. In addition they will be presented with more chronic conditions, congenital abnormalities, hernias, cancers, and 'lumps and bumps'. If they are not operated upon the patient will be left to suffer and possibly die.

Inappropriate specialist training overseas for poor world doctors (often with donor scholarship schemes) has meant that many cannot return to their home countries. The facilities for their specialist work do not exist in poor hospitals, and sometimes they do return and set up unaffordable units which become white elephants. A kidney dialysis unit was set up by Palace command in Malawi and technicians trained abroad. A few patients were treated at great cost before the machines broke or were rendered unusable by the AIDS epidemic, most died.

Often inappropriate hi-tech equipment has been donated – a CAT scan in a country where it is sometimes impossible to take an X-Ray is now available! Any repair to this sort of equipment involves flying technicians up from South Africa at great expense. Throughout Malawi much hospital equipment lies idle for want of expertise and spare parts.

Similarly, more problems arise with the demands of new technology over staff management. An intensive care unit created another dilemma. Was it right to withdraw nurses from already desperately under-staffed wards to treat, and give a better chance of life, to one or two in intensive care and allow that many more unnecessarily die on the ward as a result? The crowded male surgical ward often had over ninety patients, many very sick, and only two nurses on duty at night.

Once I entered the four bedded intensive care unit with its usual beeping of monitoring instruments. There was a slightly different, higher pitched, more continuous noise, – its origin was a box of newly hatched chicks chirping away under sister's desk. In common with many health workers, she had this side line to enable her to support her family. It was some relief to a night call !

In-patient specialist units have been set up in Malawi for treating strokes, head injuries, paralysis and cerebral palsy. If untreated, some of these patients will improve naturally, but many will die. Initial funding came from abroad but staff and scarce local resources are absorbed in such mini 'centres of excellence'. When it is realized that £3 is the amount spent per head per year on health in Malawi, (in UK it is £700), any available funds should be spent on supporting the present struggling 'centres of function' – the hospitals.

Malawi Against Polio (MAP) set up by Rotary International and funded as a charity has helped many to become mobile in an appropriate way. After an announcement at a church service, sixty seven cripples hidden away in huts in the bush came to see me at the first rural MAP clinic in 1981. Thousands of disabled children have since been helped by a system of mobile rural and town clinics. Physiotherapists, clinical officers, and doctors assess patients and crutches, calipers, and wheel chairs are made. Deformed limbs are manipulated and straightened by operation. However a child is very adaptable and will devise ways of using functioning muscles and bones to take over useless ones. The movements may appear odd but it is often unwise to try and get things to 'look right', especially in adults.

This was so with Arthur, 35 years old and paralysed as a child by polio. One contracted leg he slung behind his neck, and the other he put in a sling, so his bottom could sway freely between his arms. He insisted that he wanted to walk upright, knowing it would involve a long hospital stay. And so his contracted muscles were cut, bones broken, and joints set to allow his legs to be straightened out. When all had healed, iron callipers were fitted to allow him to bear weight in place of his useless muscles.

He struggled manfully to manage a 'swing through' gait using crutches. He was now so high off the ground and fearful of falling, that after many weeks we all admitted defeat. But he could now no longer sling his legs up and return to his previous crab like motion. I accompanied him home in a Land-Rover. He lived in a village on the steep edge of the Rift Valley, on the Shire escarpment so he could not use a wheel chair. We had to walk the final two hundred yards, but he was carried shoulder high by the rejoicing villagers. Their favourite story teller had returned, and they would have entertainment again that evening.

When the Medical School started at QE in 1991, surgical subspecialists slowly arrived in orthopaedics, neurosurgery, and plastic surgery as well as the pre-existing eye surgery. Even so there is only one surgeon per million people; whereas in Britain the figure is one per 30,000. For most of the past twenty years there has only been one doctor anaesthetist in the country. To continue the depressing comparisons, in Britain there is one qualified doctor to every 600 of the population, but in Malawi the ratio is only one doctor or clinical officer per 30,000 people; and the supply is not keeping pace with the population increase, let alone the increasing disease load.

A few decades ago, all poor world surgeons were generalists, similar to the situation in Europe in 1900. They were able to deal with anything that came their way, limited by their workload, inclinations, and facilities. I am happy to belong to this broader 'jack of all trades' team, whilst admiring the masters in the subspecialities – which developed later. For me the experience of the tissues and pathologies of every part of the body has provided a rich professional interest, and a wide appreciation of the wonders of healing.

The most rewarding aspect of my labours in a quarter of a century has lain in clinical teaching of staff, including doctors, clinical officers, medical assistants, and nurses. It is in the day-to-day hands on management of patients that professional skills are learned and they take this competence to the care of the sick in hospitals and clinics all over Malawi.

Chapter 3. The Poor

"A man cannot be rich if he has poor relatives" - Sena proverb

In our two decades in Malawi, we have witnessed not rural progress and development, but worsening poverty, malnutrition, and land degradation. The high birthrate of more than seven children per woman, coupled with infant survival policies like immunization, free food, and clean water projects, as well as oral rehydration campaigns, has caused the human population to double in eighteen years. There has been little thought for the future of these infants. 'Child survival' may be a sacred cow until one sees its bones showing through the skin.

Projects to prevent measles and diarrhoea may have saved some lives but, with the high fertility rate, they have also increased the widespread malnutrition. This has been the predictable result of infant survival campaigns without birth control: and, since health cannot be imposed on malnutrition, diseases like TB, pneumonia and malaria, and meningitis, are now flourishing.

Unchanging Scene

An industrialized economy might be able to absorb this population increase of a young generation. However a poor agricultural one like Malawi has not been able to do so. This continuing impoverishment was obvious in the Lower Shire (pronounced Shirree) Valley, lying in the southern end of the Great Rift Valley of Africa, where the mighty Shire River flows from Lake Malawi down to the Zambesi River.

The lower course of this River widens into the Elephant Marshes, where thousands of wild nyala, water buck, black rhinos, hippos, lions, and elephants once used to live. The last surviving elephant here was shot by poachers in 1989, and his skull is displayed in Majete Park.

It was interesting to compare the modern crowded and dusty situation of this valley with David Livingstone's exploratory observations in 1859. Then, he described thriving agricultural villages set in indigenous forests supporting thousands of wild animals:-

January 1859 - We steamed up the Shire ....a very great quantity of tobacco is cultivated along the banks of the river. We passed many fishing baskets moored by strong ropes, and many traps for killing hippos. Villages are very numerous and great quantities of tobacco, pumpkins, ochra, mandioc, rice, buaze, beans, and millet are cultivated. We saw several herds of elephants. At one time eight hundred were in sight.

The first comments I heard about the economic and ecological deterioration happening in rural Malawi came from my University students, ever fearful of government brutality if they reported it openly. One described his own Paiwa Village by the Shire River near Chikwawa in 1984, where the population had already doubled in twenty years to 250,000, and would rise to 370,000 by 1990:

There has been a rapid human population increase. Farmers are felling trees either for firewood, or clearing the land for their own families, or else abandoning exhausted gardens for new ones. The previous gardens are then turned into cattle and goat grazing pastures until they are devoid of plant life. The numbers of cattle in Chikwawa have trebled to 90,000 recently in addition to 60,000 goats.

One man in my village has three wives and seventeen children. He is proud of his big family. When asked about family planning, he said he would not allow his wives to practise it. Imagine how much fuel wood he needs each day and how much land he uses to produce enough food! People travel long distances to collect firewood, often crossing into Mozambique.

When farmers were asked why they did not plant trees to replace the felled ones, they replied 'Thango yake ninje? Kusowa bara kweko?' which in Sena means 'What for? Are you short of work?' In strong winds, a cloud of dust rises high in the sky so that people stop walking, afraid of dust and flying pebbles. In Sena custom, a man purchases a bride with payments of cattle. This encourages polygamy. A man with money and cattle can buy many wives. By having large families, the people of the Lower Shire are digging their own graves. The valley is beginning to turn to desert.

Another student commented on his own polygamous home area in Chikwawa in 1985:

If the population continues to grow at its present rate, people in Chikwawa area will be hungrier, dirtier, more crowded, and more quarrelsome, and the environment will continue to be wrecked. Malawi should strive at least to achieve a low birthrate by whatever means available to its citizens. The longer we wait to tackle the population problem, the more damage will be forced on our district. We shall then adjust the hard way by catastrophe, instead of by calculation.

I had to hide these student reports, and dozens more like it, behind my ball gown in our bedroom wardrobe. These ideas were not acceptable to Dr. Banda's regime which followed the policies advised by foreign aid donors and the United Nations Agencies. Young Malawian men, who could perceive their own national problems, faced punishment if they were seen to criticize official policies.

During Michael's regular surgical visits to hospitals in Chikwawa for eighteen years, we too saw the steady deterioration in the quality of life in the Shire Valley. On one occasion during the crackling dry season in 1988, we drove three thousand feet down the steep Rift Valley escarpment road, with panoramic views of the Shire River down in the valley below us, a shining silver thread bordered with green.

At Chikwawa town on the Shire riverside, where the most of the old shops had been boarded up since the Asians were forcibly moved out twenty years previously, we found lorries unloading maize sacks. The district commissioner said the grain was a gift from Britain and the European Union for famished villagers, and lorries heavy with maize were arriving daily. The German ambassador was coming to donate more vehicles, as well as two canvas grain silos which were being erected outside the hospital and grass-fenced prison. For several years the majority of the people living in the Lower Shire Valley were supplied with free food by foreign donors. But in 1997, the World Food Programme pulled out of such programmes because twenty years of food aid had led to no health improvements. These people were then cruelly abandoned.

Michael's hospital surgical lists at Chikwawa also indicated the problems of diseases that thrive on poverty and malnutrition - bladder cancer related to bilharzia which spreads as ever more crowds of people live by the marshes, elephantiasis caused by filariasis, orthopaedic deformities due to bone TB which thrives in malnutrition, and cervical cancer which has a higher incidence where there is crowded promiscuity..

He saw another tragic victim of the local struggle for survival writing: "A pale sweating young man lay in the ward, his sheet kept from his legs by a wire cage. A musky mousy smell hung around, and the spongy feel of his thigh gave the diagnosis of gas gangrene. He had been bitten by a crocodile five days before while he was getting into his dugout canoe to fish in a marshy area of the Shire River.

His only chance was amputation at the thigh but he was too anaemic to stand an anaesthetic. So we tried to get blood but, perhaps mercifully, he died before the last booked operation on my list. There was a feeling of relief in theatre, perhaps it was better to die on the ward than in a vain attempt on the operating table." Afterwards I was curious to read David Livingstone's statement that *The Shire fishermen say that when crocodiles can easily obtain an abundance of fish, they rarely attack men.* Perhaps this man too was a victim of the overfishing of this River.

The old British colonial hospital at Chikwawa was surrounded by trees shedding leaves, yellowy grass, and little black pigs diging up roots. I walked around the wards seeing so many weary, barefoot, ragged, people - mothers wearing only a sack around the waist, with thin sagging breasts, often with moaning yellow babies clutching at these breasts in the small hope of food. These infants must be thirsty as well as starving. The TB-HIV patients in striped shirts sat outside in the sunshine with goats baaing around them. The wards were crowded and badly under-staffed with often only one nurse to manage a hundred and eighty patients at night. A new kitchen and wards were being built by UNHCR and workmen were making a fire of the sweet smelling, old,

Mulanje cedar door frames to boil their maize for lunch.

On one of our visits, during lunch with the hospital doctor in his delapidated colonial house which had a ruined swimming pool, we looked down on five huge hippos sitting on a mud bank in the cool River, and heard the fish eagles calling in the great heat of noon. He commented on the grave problems of the area - "These people are not at all interested in health education, it is all so boring to hear. Nobody wants to dig pit latrines!"

However he pointed out that one human message did seem popular in Chikwawa. The tiny local Catholic bookshop had apparently sold dozens of copies of my little marriage and contraception book, and wanted more because, as the bookseller said, "women in Chikwawa do not find happiness or sexual fulfillment in their polygamous marriages. That is why everybody wants to read your booklet." It is interesting that a moral idea of sex, marriage and parenthood, struck a chord in this poor area. The pioneer Christian missionaries a century ago perhaps offered more inspiration to a polygamous culture than the health and development theorists today. The British High Commissioner paid for the printing of this booklet from his aid fund. It has since been translated into Chichewa and is still in great demand all over Malawi.

This news was gratifying, and it is not surprising that organizations like Marie Stopes International have had more success in pioneering birth control than health lobbies, when they were at last allowed to open in the Lower Shire Valley by 1990. After the morning surgical list at Chikwawa, we drove twenty miles down the sandy Shire Valley, passing many brilliant crimson and blue carmine bee eaters and a Dickinson's kestrel perched on the collapsing telephone lines.

At the fee paying Nchalo Catholic Mission Hospital, the well-watered gardens, shady trees, peaceful grounds, and smart nurses, seemed like an oasis in this sandy terrain. Whilst Michael operated with the clinical officer on a patient seriously injured by a hippo, the Malawian Sisters kindly invited me to coffee. Catholic convents always offer a heartening welcome.

They said one problem was the large number of mother-supported families in the Lower Shire Valley, because polygamy did not create strong emotional bonds between spouses. Once father left home the children suffered. This meant that many people had little food. But in this Catholic district the mothers were trapped in their own fertility. They had no escape from continual pregnancies and the consequent malnutrition.

It led me to think that if European Catholics do want to help African families, they could do no better than try to change their Church's official policy on contraception. Women living in Catholic hospital areas have no access to birth control which would lead them to have fewer babies, and keep their husbands sexually faithful. After all, a man in a satisfying matrimonial/sexual relationship will probably be emotionally interested in his wife and children, keen to maintain and guide them, and this is the corner-stone of human survival.

Perhaps these emotional problems of rural Africa pose a challenge to all the consumerism and dispassionate gender egalitarianism of the Western world. Normal human instincts and matrimony need to be accorded more respect by rich world politicians and academic aid theorists. Two of the four hospitals, with all their out-reach health centres, in the Lower Shire Valley are Catholic, which means that half the inhabitants of this destitute district have limited possibilities of improving their lives. Such poverty cannot be alleviated, let alone eradicated, until the birthrate is reduced.

The Malawian clinical officer at the hospital said he too was worried about this area. Patients were so dulled by poverty that they could often not answer simple questions. They were an exhausted people. The rains were now becoming less predictable and the land was as exhausted. There are degrees of poverty and a scale could be devised. People in such a situation become apathetic about just surviving. It is not possible for them to make plans or undertake projects. They know they are the victims of fate, of the capricious rains, of witchcraft, of foreign aid policies.

In 1989, doctors told us of their Shire Valley nutrition survey. Whilst babies with 'kwashiorkor' are the victims of recent dietary inadequacy, stunted children have never received enough food. They are the victims of long term shortages. "Throughout the southern region of Malawi over one third of children are severely stunted by six months of age" - in lay terms this meant that malnourished mothers had not enough breast milk.

Our private emotions in all this sorrow were fragmented. We could only help by persisting in a deteriorating situation; but we felt sad anger at the rich world's lack of perception, and at the academic false optimism prevalent in Britain and America in defining African problems. Official talk of 'poverty eradication' sounds crazy in Chikwawa district. Educated Malawian young men were in fact prevented from defining their nation's problems by the remote colonialism of rich donor governments. However, in the end, it will be these educated males who will determine the future of their nation and the rest of the world should respect this.

Nonetheless the beautiful landscape of the Lower Shire Valley diverted us, and maintained our spirits in the scale of such human tragedy. We often escaped into the thrilling natural beauty of this Rift Valley. During one walk up the Zulu tributary of the Shire in the January summer storms, we witnessed fishermen throwing weighted circular nets into the marshy waters where electric fish were caught, Pied kingfishers flying rapidly and low across the river, and a tree frog's nest on a branch overhanging a backwater pool with a frothy cocoon from which tadpoles fell into the water. Black clouds darkened the summer January sky as we walked back in heavy and pelting rain.

I remember too the Shire Valley in October, the winter dry season, as I described in my diary: "Grass fires were raging across the nearby hillsides, fanned by the wind. On the edge of the fire several fearless Drongo birds were flying low over the grass, from tree to tree. They were catching the insects rising from the heat. The dark blue Drongos, brilliant yellow grass, blazing flames, and rust coloured leaves were set against the distant blue hills".

During a trip down another tributary of the Shire, the Luchenya river, in Mulanje district in April 1989, I wrote "It is the end of the summer rains, and there are signs of the massive flood waters that have been pouring off Mulanje mountain recently. As we float down, maize cobs are hanging twelve feet above us in the trees, sighing bamboos are flattened to the ground and raffia palms are bent over. The river water is still above normal levels, and in our little blow-up rubber boat, we career over endless rapids. I have never, in one day, floated over more cascading waterfalls. The river flows off the steep granite slopes of Mulanje Mountain so the current is very strong.

We are not alone. Dozens of ragged children run along the river banks to greet us, waving in excitement at the strange sight of a rubber boat and 'mzungus' (whites). Michael points out the yellow palms of their waving hands - due to having survived only on mangoes for many weeks now.

After two hours, we reach Chief Mabuka's village, where I sit for an hour with our boat whilst Michael walks to fetch our car. Everyone comes out to sit beside me, with the kindness that is characteristic of the poor. It seems about fifty children and five adults live here. Just one speaks English. Most are wearing a few rags. Many have pot bellies and the thinning discoloured hair that indicates malnutrition. One little boy creeps beside me, with pale dry skin and puffed closing eyelids, almost too weak to sit up. He looks close to death. When Michael arrives, he points out that many children who look like four-year olds are probably stunted ten or eleven-year olds. The people tell us that Chief Mabuka has thirty six villages in this area and there are now far too many people and not enough food."

A few weeks later a Mulanje Chief's granddaughter in my Polytechnic class told me, in great fear, how chiefs of starving villagers were beaten by Banda's government officials if they ever complained of food shortages and that, despite the danger of imprisonment, she wanted to study her district and raise the hunger issue. She planned to interview fifty families and shopkeepers who would trust her because she was one of them. She completed her investigations and handed me her project full of fear. I hid it in my bottom drawer.

Another young man gave me his similar essay in 1988 with a telling observation - *You see Mrs. King it has been a relief to me to write this truthful report on my own village. We Malawian young men are never allowed to see, to perceive, to analyse, or even to think about what is wrong here in Africa. It causes us personal stress to live with the delusions thrust on us by politicians and foreign donors. For years I have had to repress my perception of the real world around me, and it has been like a Freudian relief for me just to write this essay. But if anyone knows what I think, my whole family may be in terrible trouble.*

Foreign aid to African countries has reversed the principle of 'no taxation without representation'. Many educated young Malawians see the solution to their country's problems lies in a national population policy and a new kind of marriage and family life - such as one of 'one wife and two children'. But they are over-ruled by the dogmas of foreign donor governments and the United Nations agencies.

The political tune in Malawi is called by the voters in Europe and America who cannot perceive the reality of African life. European television viewers promote child survivalism by responding immediately to the pictures of crisis and disaster, oblivious of polygamy and the high birthrates which are the cruxes of this 'real poverty'.

In 1989, the dozen British Aid doctors in Malawi were invited to the British High Commission in Lilongwe to discuss future health policy. Aid was politically committed to community medicine and child survival. Most of these doctors vainly pointed out that the underlying deterioration in health and the increasing malnutrition was due to the population increase, and this situation would become worse with such programmes.

Firewood for the Town

But British government aid policy is determined by the attitudes of voters at home and not by the first hand experience of doctors working in African hospitals. So these honest, uncomfortable, medical words were not acceptable, and the fairy-tale concepts of "Health for All" continued. Community medicine professors, have been too glib with their ready-made recipes for improving African health. The real problem lies in the fact that if they have not first identifed the demographic problem, they have a flawed solution.

Poverty, malnutrition, and disease, have worsened every year. In 1993 our Queen Elizabeth hospital was having to refuse to admit some starving children because there were already so many infants per cot. By 1994, with the maize stores empty, villagers in many areas of Malawi were often abandoning their homes and trekking off to forage leaves, grass, and roots, to eat: they were becoming ecological refugees. We heard the BBC report of three million people starving in south Malawi, only a million more than usual, was the grim comment.

Eventually Michael's exasperation with this crisis gave rise to a versified outrage:

> "There was a stunted man, who had a stunted wife,
> And they both lived together a little stunted life,
> Their little stunted stomachs survived on what they got,
> Just as well they're stunted, because they didn't get a lot.
> But when the little baby
> Inside the mother's womb,
> Grew too large for her pelvis,
> It became its stunted tomb.
>
>
> For those who have to survive and suffer,
> And remain to bear the brunt
> Of the next international child survival,
> Safer motherhood, or cleaner water stunt -
> So they're forced to ravish the land and strip the trees
> Because they're already too many; won't the donors please,
> Ensure that what next onto the poor is shunted
> Makes them a little better off, or only moderately stunted."

It's an exasperation which has seen no alleviation.

Chapter 4. The AIDS Epidemic

Every aspect of life and work in Malawi has been undermined by the catastrophic HIV epidemic with mortality akin to the European Black Death of 1348 . Recently the staff of a Catholic AIDS support group told me: "Today there is little light at the end of the tunnel of distress. Every week sees an increase in the numbers of patients suffering and dying of HIV, and every month more bereaved families with little to live on. Soon, extended families will not be able to look after the numbers of AIDS orphans (over a million by 1999)."

Looking back, it is difficult to imagine the time before this disease affected everybody in Malawi. Letters sent home to our daughters revealed our first fears:

"October 1985 - The rains have already come and the land is changing from brown to green. A pair of long eared owls in our garden have hatched nestlings. I have seen, with help, over 100 outpatients in my clinic today, including the first laboratory confirmed case of AIDS here - Dad."

"1 November 1985 - it is very hot now, 87'F on our verandah. There are unending problems at the hospital. Yesterday Dad told me he would be operating on his first patient with AIDS, and asked if it would worry me? After tea, he walked across the lawn to look at a baby owl in its nest on the ground. The male owl swooped down on him from the tree above, and scratched his head with its talons, drawing blood. How much we have to worry about now - Mummy."

The Owl Swoops

10 November 1985 "I am just back from climbing Ndirande mountain with three British medical students - there was a baboon barking on the peak. A cloud of flying termites has appeared after the first rains. Next week we go to a surgeon's meeting in Tanzania to read a paper Mum and I have written about Kaposi's Sarcoma in Malawi. For many years there have been about twenty five biopsied male patients yearly with this cancer, and we have now seen five AIDS-related cases in one month - Dad."

AIDS was first manifest in Blantyre, revealing itself by the increasing numbers of cases of this curious cancer, Kaposi's Sarcoma, which produces a bluish nodularity of the legs in men, spreading slowly over many years. Suddenly it was presenting on other sites of the body including the mouth. This HIV-cancer is more aggressive, also occurs in women, spreads fast in the body, and, often involving the vital organs, leads to death. The HIV-virus encountered in Malawi was probably lurking in a few people for two decades before this epidemic flowered exponentially and internationally, as these statistics from the John Hopkins' research project show:

HIV Seroprevalence Rate for Pregnant Mothers in Blantyre

1985	2%	1992	27%
1986	3%	1993	30%
1987	8%	1994	32%
1988	19%	1995	33%
1990	22%	1996	35%
1991	26%	1997	37%

These statistics, derived from our Queen Elizabeth hospital in Blantyre, testing the blood of the expectant mothers in the ante-natal clinic, were not given to the general public in Malawi until 1994. The incidence levelled slightly in the nineties possibly because the exit rate by death was beginning to equal the entry rate of people becoming infected.

Most research tested the blood of pregnant women. However an increasing number of HIV-positive ladies complained of secondary amenorrhoea and infertility. So it would seem that if females in concentration camps, and athletes, tend to stop menstruating, then it is likely that AIDS also depletes human fertility. It also means that the official AIDS figures derived from tests on pregnant women may be less than the general population prevalence of HIV.

An interesting sex/age difference was reported at a clinical meeting of the Malawi Medical Association in 1989. Of HIV-patients dying under the age of thirty years, 80% were female, but men predominated in the over-thirties patients. Overall equal numbers were dying in both sexes. There was lively banter at a dinner afterwards when elderly, male, British Dr.B. commented that if HIV was spreading between younger women and older men, there was only one reason - money!

However rural hospitals suggested a different gender picture in the villages; one hospital reported an HIV-baby, losing weight and with deep skin ulcers, being carried in by a ten year old girl saying - "this baby's mother is my sister aged fourteen, and she is sick with AIDS in the ward." Father was alleged to be a local official who had made several village girls pregnant and given them HIV too. Old tribal initiation ceremonies often required adolescent girls to confirm their adult status in promiscuous rituals, and this was a likely result.

Whilst Malawian hospital staff could see the grave dangers of this epidemic, with clinics and wards filling with suffering victims, politicians and diplomats were reluctant to admit the problem in the eighties. News of this rapidly spreading disease was cloaked in official secrecy by the government, which meant that I gleaned information from social sources.

The comments of doctors made over our dinner table were a fascinating record of a disease disaster. I noted them in my diary, passing on the information to university students who would write the word "AIDS" on a piece of paper in front of me because it was politically treacherous to mention it; then I would quietly tell them the latest news. They had an intelligence network although they had no say in Malawian problems, and AIDS policies for Africa were decided by United Nations agencies like the World Health Organization or the donor governments.

On a winter July afternoon, when Michael was expecting war casualities from Mozambique, including both soldiers and civilians with gunshot wounds, a British medical student from Cambridge came to play string music with us and enjoy hot crumpets and honey for tea.

He was working with the physicians in Queen Elizabeth hospital, and told of the galloping rate of herpes (shingles) patients in the medical clinics. There were over eight hundred cases in the first seven months of 1987, whilst only three years previously two hundred had been diagnosed in a whole year. This was a good indicator of the exponential progress of AIDS and other sexually transmitted diseases. This news too was passed on to my students.

If the aim of development is to prevent disease and achieve 'Health for All', then the foreign policies about HIV have proved expensive and ineffective. Politically correct attitudes about race, gender, and human private rights, in the rich Western world certainly took precedence over safeguarding innocent adults and unborn children from AIDS in East Africa.

When the problem is mainly confined to a few homosexuals and drug abusers in a hospital clinic in Britain, the general heterosexual public and unborn children are not much threatened by the disease. Instead individuals can claim the right not to be HIV-tested or labelled as HIV-positive.

However these British 'human rights' were sadly imposed by foreign community medicine experts on the far worse epidemic in Africa, which protected the rights of infected persons, and indeed their right to spread this deadly virus. Basically people were not allowed to perceive the high levels of HIV-infection in Central Africa as a global danger.

Not until Dr. Banda had fallen from power in 1994, were full local HIV statistics announced to the general public at a rally in Blantyre. But then it was too late to put the clock back. Once a third of an adult community carries this HIV virus, the spread of this disease cannot be easily controlled by any campaigns.

Privately we tried to alert diplomats to the dangers of the epidemic, but they too were pressurized by public attitudes from home. For instance, in 1987, we were invited to sample the delicious wine, but not such good modern art, at the French ambassador's leaving party. The Swedish ambassador came up and asked us very courteously how a million dollars could be spent on AIDS in Africa? We replied that Malawian doctors had just been forbidden by Dr. Banda's government to mention the national HIV-figures at a World Health Organization conference, and that when the African Director of WHO came to Malawi, he had not been allowed to have access to these statistics.

The WHO was pussy-footing about the AIDS issue, with well heeled officials more keen to preserve their own jobs than offend African rulers by publicizing this epidemic. Polishing the image of dictators, took precedence over frightening but educating the general population about the dangers of this disease.

This peculiar blindness to HIV seemed to be universal, and linked to ancient prejudices about sexual behaviour. The old male libertarian world was a paradise lost with HIV! Poetry and novels would have to change! When a visiting American surgeon came to our dinner of fried chambo with pumpkin, he mentioned that liberals in San Francisco had formed a political lobby against AIDS-prevention measures. They had even opposed HIV-testing blood donated for transfusion in surgery.

He went on to query whether HIV-infected persons should have the human right to spread this terrible disease to the innocent who are still free of it. Western governments have have so far ducked this issue, being terrified of 'discriminating', even in order to prevent an epidemic of such a terrible lethal disease.

Denial of the disease characterized patients too. In the blooming rose gardens around our Queen Elizabeth hospital, with Soche mountain rising steeply behind, Malawian clinicians nervously described their frequent and awful task of counselling the parents of well-to-do AIDS children.

A typical mother brought her husband in to be HIV-tested and he was positive. She then wept in anger, saying "I have not been with other men, it is your fault that we all have AIDS. You have been visiting girlfriends and caught it, and have caused us all now to be dying".

By December 1987, some HIV figures were at last admitted quietly to doctors and civil servants in Lilongwe. A telegram arrived at this meeting from the World Health Organization in Geneva -'how many condoms does Malawi need?' WHO spent large sums on showering East Africa with condoms and safe sex messages, which arguably gave many people encouragement to indulge in risky behaviour and catch AIDS.

Condoms are not entirely safe even as contraceptives, although a sperm is two hundred times larger than the HIV virus, and a woman is usually fertile for only forty eight hours a month. There is presumably a considerably higher risk of catching the much smaller HIV-virus when using condoms - on any day of the month!

Even a 'New Scientist' review in 1993 concluded that 'there is scant evidence that more condoms means less AIDS'. Nonetheless, the international donors' expenditure on condoms was, and is, ethically justifiable: people have a right to use them. And to be fair, foreign governments have also made commendable efforts to supply Malawian hospitals with extra rubber gloves, syringes, and test-kits to screen blood for HIV, which have been most gratefully received.

The millions of dollars of international taxpayers' money spent on WHO and UNICEF workshops to discuss HIV though, was rather more wasted than effective because it did not apparently slow this disease in Malawi; these workshops did, of course, keep well salaried WHO officials in good jobs. They had to be seen to spend their budget, even if the health information from Europe and US had little appeal in African culture. I wrote about this typical workshop, out of dozens going on all the time in African countries, in my diary:

"November 1988 - We found the hotel beside Lake Malawi was full of government cars and scores of civil servants and hospital staff attending an AIDS workshop organized by the World Health Organization. This is how WHO funds are spent - providing barbecue lunches on the beach, luxury dinners, drinks, weekend hotel accommodation, free transport, and of course 'per diem' money for each person attending. They are here to talk about HIV all day. However the many painted ladies already gathering around the approach road, indicate that WHO funds do rather more than cause participants to talk about AIDS.

These workshops also continually deprive hospitals of vital senior staff. For instance, our pharmacist, trained in France, is also attending. Like his predecessors, he is not working in our pharmacy very often, because he is seduced by the high per diems offered by WHO, UNICEF, and UNDP, to be off at workshops much of the time - Brazzaville one week, Nairobi another; he is now enjoying a sumptious weekend here beside the lake."

Even more sad was the expenditure by the World Health Organization on huge international HIV conferences, when African hospitals were so deprived of funds to cater for victims. For instance, the Amsterdam AIDS conference of 1992 was attended by twelve thousand delegates and was estimated by the 'New Scientist' magazine in all to cost twenty-five million US dollars - was it aiming to advocate safe debauchery! Meanwhile, the agonizing plight of thousands of dying HIV patients was provided with little succour.

We also heard complaints from Malawian clinicians and university students that the American AIDS and reproductive health messages were not respected or wanted by local Africans. It is doubtful whether the 'safe sex with condoms' propaganda achieved much, if anything at all. In 1996 the Malawi government commented officially that although 98% of the people knew all about AIDS, traditional sexual behaviour had in no way changed. Foreigners did not understand the nut that must be cracked - the hoary old polygamous morality.

The World Bank reported in 1996 *Many Malawian women accept multiple sexual partners as normal behaviour for males, although they do not like it. Among women multiple partners are much less common.*

Liberal sexual and homosexual lobbies in both Houses of the British Parliament have opposed HIV-testing, although many countries, such as India, Taiwan and Australia HIV-screened foreign students before they were allowed to take up scholarships for university courses.

In 1993, Baroness Cumberlege, the British Secretary of State for Health wrote: *We do not wish to discriminate against people who are HIV-infected and we would not want to refuse a person higher education on these grounds.* So large sums of British taxpayers' money were then spent on bringing students infected with the African HIV-virus to study in Britain, who soon died after returning to East Africa.

For example, at least four doctors trained in London at a cost of £100,000 each to the British taxpayer, died of AIDS after a few months of service back in Malawi. This money could have been better spent on healthy Malawian students to return to help their country in the hour of AIDS crisis. The Catholic church of Malawi requires seminarians to be HIV-tested before starting a long training as priests. We believe that scarce university places in Malawi should also require a health certificate.

Despite all this, there was little help for the ever-increasing numbers of patients suffering with AIDS in hospitals. In fact, in 1987 hospital budgets were cut and annual reductions in health expenditure occurred over the next decade, due to the declining Malawian economy.

I recall some surgical dinner guests in 1988 expressing more frustration about international attitudes. They had arrived when the first November rains had fallen, after seven months of drought and intense searing sunshine, the smell of the damp ground was a pungent relief. Outside our drawing room window a chorus of crickets, ciccadas, and frogs were singing in the newly damp ditches. Even the full moon was dim in the passing clouds.

Against this freshened backdrop, these visiting doctors appreciated the comforts of our home and dinner table after the harsh sorrows they had seen during the day. A gynaecologist said the women in our Queen Elizabeth hospital were the poorest and saddest she had seen in Africa.

Half of these wards were then full of AIDS patients and these ladies did not quite fit into any of the international clinical definitions of AIDS issued by the World Health Organization. In Blantyre, they were increasingly thin and had genital ulcers which would not heal; very slowly as the ulceration progressed, they died in much pain as palliative drugs like morphia were in very short supply.

Of the mothers tested in her clinic, 25% were HIV-positive by 1988. This doctor said the WHO was still suggesting that AIDS was a risk of prostitution whereas she saw that it was widely prevalent in the normal family community. But the WHO seemed rarely to respond to clinicians. Instead it wasted money sending her unrealistic 'AIDS Advice' printed in expensive glossy booklets.

Whilst she worried about her ward, the advisors' remit did not concern the plight of HIV-patients crowding out African hospitals. The labour ward usually had fifteen or more mothers in labour, and there were not enough sheets to provide a clean one for each patient. There was blood all over the place and often a lack of disinfectant or bleach to clean it, together with dire shortages of sutures, drugs and dressings.

Of course doctors worried about catching AIDS in their work. One doctor asked to be tested after accidentally pricking himself with a lumbar puncture needle when taking spinal fluid from an AIDS baby, another after having blood spurted in her face when delivering an HIV-infected mother. Luckily none of these doctors were infected and it seems to be quite difficult for health staff to catch AIDS in their work. But there are some documented cases.

Michael usually tried to wear two pairs of gloves when operating. In Malawi, these gloves were re-used (resterilized) disposable ones and were often perforated. Needing to wear glasses, he is always surprised at how many small blood and fluid droplets get on to them even during a 'bloodless' procedure. We decided that as our children were grown up, we must not live in fear of him catching HIV from surgery on hundreds of AIDS patients in the course of fifteen years. So far, he remains negative.

But by the nineties the spectre of this disease became horrendous in the poorest villages beside the Shire River, where in the searing midday heat hippos and crocodiles lurked in the water. As the HIV epidemic rapidly increased the numbers of moribund patients in Chikwawa hospital, so the great reaper also harvested members of the clinical staff. In 1993 we heard that so many patients were dying of AIDS at Chikwawa hospital that relatives were no longer coming to collect some dead bodies for burial, because most adults in the family had already perished; now these AIDS riddled corpses were left decomposing in the great heat of the hospital mortuary.

When convicts from the next door prison were asked to bury them, they appealed against this request to the International Committee of the Red Cross, which promptly ruled that such work was an abuse of prisoners' human rights. 'Let the dead bury their dead' was what they proclaimed. All these extra tragic problems were of course relegated to the struggling and over-burdened hospital staff.

Statistics hid the pain of AIDS. I was distressed to encounter a patient lying in a Malawian district hospital, who indicated the needs of thousands of HIV-patients for palliative care. I saw a polygamous wife in the postnatal ward, who could still not be discharged from hospital five weeks after childbirth due to septicaemia; she lay on her bed in pain, her hair thinning and her face bleaching as the skin peeled off her, layer after layer; her caesararian scar would not heal, having gone septic immediately after delivery and she had returned to theatre three times to have it stitched up again. But the tissues would not unite because of AIDS, which allowed the infection to spread to her whole abdomen - an open mass of pus. It was certain that she would die in a slow agony, and her baby would then lose his food supply and perish as well. It was tragic to see.

She was a victim of so many horrible belief systems - of polygamy, of cultural pressures for human fertility, of 'pro-life religious lobbies' which fundamentally oppose abortion even if mother and baby both died in

River below Chikwawa

such conditions, and of the failure of the rich world to inspire a human morality that could be respected in African poverty.

Women are sometimes thought to be the moral guardians of society and as such some are speaking out in both Christian groups and womens' rights lobbies in Malawi, demanding new one-wife marriage laws.

Recently I met a nurse who had seen eleven of her friends die after marrying HIV-infected men: *Most of my best friends from school and my nursing course are now in their graves. Often the first sign of this disease was a miscarriage or the baby dying. Then the mother sickened with symptoms like TB, ulcers, or cancer, and a long worsening illness got its grip. Father usually survived longest, and twice I have seen a widower remarry and repeat again.*

I decided I would not catch AIDS a long time ago, when I saw patients dying in the hospital wards. If a man makes advances to me, I say to him, have you had an HIV-test? Then he goes off and does not return; but I am still alive, and I treasure my life.

Chapter 5.   A Century of Surgery   MK

The first recorded surgical encounter in these lands, was in June 1863. This is from a contemporary account of Livingstone's Zambesi expedition, as his exploring party travelled up the Shire River towards Lake Nyasa.

Fleeing for their lives and hotly pursued, they reached the river bank about a cables' length ahead of our vessel, and plunged into the river. The woman in question, less fortunate than others, was struck down by an arrow as she rose to the surface. Entering just below the left shoulder blade, the cruelly barbed head passed into her lungs; and when Dr. Livingstone, Dr. Kirk, and Dr. Mellor, saw her afterwards, it was decided by this council of surgeons that the attempt to extricate it would only add to her terrible sufferings, and cause her more speedy death. Extraordinary to relate, the men of the village took upon themselves to do that which no one better versed in such matters dare justify for a minute. Fastening a piece of string to the iron head, they drew it back by main force, cutting off the entangled flesh from the large fang-like barbs, and actually repeating the same process as portions of the lung appeared! Our astonishment was complete the next day to find no fatal symptoms had set in. Each day I saw to her diet myself. Now she came forward (twelve years later in 1875) to greet us, bringing me a present of a fowl, and from all appearances had shaken off the ill effects of a barbarous operation in every sense of the word. (E.D.Young R.N. 'Nyasa' 1875)

Arrow injuries are less common now - I have only seen one, non-barbed arrow wound, but gunshot wounds are becoming increasingly common. The most dramatic to come to me was a very pale collapsed eight year old boy. He had been accidentally shot in the chest with a pump up air gun firing ball bearings. He had a small wound over the sternum in the centre of his chest and the X-rays showed a 'bullet' in the heart. Blood was escaping at each beat into the surrounding heart sac, accumulating and compressing the heart itself, a condition known as 'tamponade'. In theatre the sternum and heart sac were split open, blood gushed out and the heart was once again able to expand and his blood pressure improved. The small hole in the right side of the heart was stitched and the chest closed up. But we had not found the ball bearing either in the spilt blood or the heart sac.

The next day he was much better but a chest X-ray showed no sign of the bullet. It could have entered the left side of the heart after lodging in the dividing wall, and been pumped anywhere in the body, plugging the blood vessel where it ended up. Luckily it had not produced a stroke, or gangrene of the intestines or a limb. A full body X-ray was done - and there it was, behind the left knee! There was enough extra circulation to the lower leg to keep it healthy. After two days it was removed through a small incision in the artery, and he went home a week later.

In a similar way, when the lung is punctured, 'tamponade' due to air leakage occurs. During the Millenium celebrations a 20 year old man who had been stabbed was brought in by the police to a district hospital run entirely by clinical officers (paramedics), close to where I was staying. He was extremely breathless and prostrate but the most striking thing was his left chest wall and shoulder which was swollen up like a balloon by air under the skin. The small stab wound was leaking air but obviously far more air was leaking from the lung inside and compressing the lung and heart over to the right. Under local anaesthetic we inserted one end of a length of drip tubing into the chest; the other end was put into a bowl of water. Air bubbled out and so the lung could expand again and he immediately became less breathless. After a few hours the lung hole sealed itself off and there were no more bubbles. The tube was later removed and he went home.

In 1876, Dr. Robert Laws carried out the first modern surgical operation in Central Africa on his dining room table at Cape Maclear, beside Lake Nyasa. Africans stood and watched as chloroform was administered, by dripping it on to gauze held over the patient's mouth and nose; as he lay insensible, the astonishment of the audience knew no bounds. After removal of a cystic tumour above his eye, this patient recovered well. News spread far and wide and soon many more patients appeared. People called the chloroform 'dying' and would crowd around to stand in open mouthed wonder as Dr. Laws calmly cut away while his African assistants mopped up the blood. Dr. Laws commented "the sooner we get them trained to do this work, the better." He served for fifty two years, training many hospital staff.

Today ether and halothane are used instead of chloroform, and with more sophisticated apparatus. The most common anaesthetic in the poor world is probably ketamine injection, which can be used for most proceedures including Caesarian section.

Local anaesthetics are given in various ways today, as they were by the pioneers. In the early days cocaine drops and injections were often used for cataract extractions. Today only a few general surgeons in the poor world extract cataracts - my last one was twenty five years ago. There is a well trained cadre of peripatetic Ophthalmology Clinical Officers who do this work in district hospitals in Malawi. It is humbling to look through operating theatre books and see lists of over twenty cases done on one day by a single operator.

Amputations feature in early records, often as a consequence of injuries in the old tribal and anti-slavery conflicts. An open fractured limb might go on to gangrene, and amputation was often needed to save life. In the

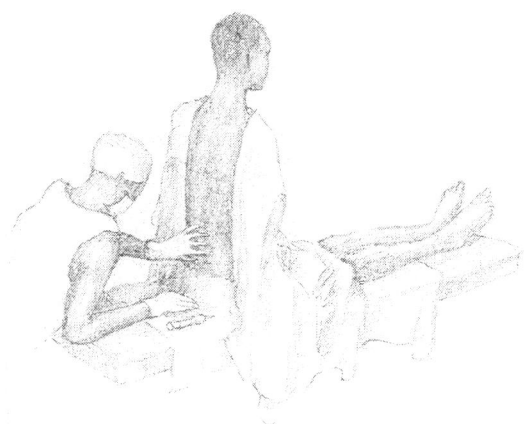

Spinal Anaesthesia

1888 British campaign against the Arab slavers in North Malawi, Lord Lugard sustained an open fracture of his arm from a bullet wound; Dr. Cross was able to save this limb by nursing him sitting up in a chair for several weeks. This was before the days of plaster of Paris and antibiotics.

In the 1930s, tubes were inserted into wounds and irrigated with disinfectant solutions, a technique occasionally used today. In the past, as now, the supply of bandages and dressings for wounds often run out or are in very short supply. We could pick up ideas from the pioneers who used sterilized sawdust and raw cotton for discharging wounds, covered with banana leaves. In 1914, appeals were sent from mission hospital staff to Britain for old sheets and table cloths to be used as bandages. Honey, sugar, and paw paw leaves were used then, as now, as a dressing for chronic ulcers and wounds slow to heal. No doubt the early doctors noted the ability of fly maggots to clean up the dead tissue in a dirty injury leaving a healthy wound. We see this in neglected wounds today but I have never deliberately introduced flies, there is usually no need. Periodically in the surgical journals this is advocated, but maggots crawl around!

Amputations for trauma today are common, although not so frequent as in neighbouring Mozambique where land mines continue their toll. Often a patient with cancer of the skin allows it to grow so large before coming to the doctor that amputation is the only choice. This was so in a forty year old woman in a district hospital. In her youth she had burnt her lower leg, which never healed properly. Over the years this had turned into a malignant ulcer, eroding into the bone, which was obviously about to fracture. She was very anaemic so was given iron and anti-hookworm pills before her operation a month later. We had sterilized the carpenter's hacksaw, but then decided on amputation through the knee joint, under a spinal anaesthetic. She recovered well and the hospital carpenter made her crutches.

Infections often lead to surgery now as in the past. Luckily diphtheria is no longer seen, due to immunization, but a tragedy of Shakespearian proportions relating to it was recorded in the Blantyre Mission reports in 1891:

A baby son of Henry Henderson, who had married Dr. Bowie's sister, caught diphtheria. The diphtheria membrane blocked his throat. In a vain attempt to save the child's life, Dr. Bowie did a tracheostomy and sucked the tube inserted into the windpipe, and caught the infection. He made all the preparations for a similar operation on himself for he was a skilled surgeon. He summoned another relative, Dr. Affleck Scott, from Mulanje Mission. The latter, to cross the Thuchilla River, swollen by torrential rains, made a bridge of bamboo from bough to bough of trees on either side. But all in vain! Bowie died and was buried beside his sister - the baby's mother who had also died. So three family diphtheria deaths occurred within nine days in January 1891. Henry Henderson, a broken man, left to take Mrs. Bowie back to Britain; but on reaching Quelimane at the mouth of the Zambesi River, they were stricken with fever, and both died there - brother in law and sister in law. Dr. Bowie had come to Blantyre from St. Bartholomew's Hospital, London.

Over a century later, I had a happier experience with a tracheostomy patient at a district hospital. The patient had a large tumour of the salivary gland below the jaw. The operation was straightforward and later in the day he was doing well. However, in the night the nurse noticed he was having difficulty in breathing due to swelling into the throat. The clinical officer was called and this patient was taken back to theatre and given oxygen. I was fetched from our home two miles away. On arrival, the patient was unconscious and we did a tracheostomy below the swelling using a piece of plastic pipe. He could now breathe through this artificial opening in his neck and soon improved. Since we had no proper tracheostomy tubes it was most important that this plastic one did not come out or become blocked by blood or mucus.

In a rich country he would have been in intensive care with one nurse per patient. As the sole nurse on night duty for the hospital was responsible for so many patients, I explained to his wife how to use the foot sucker to suck out secretions and keep the area clean. The wife said she could not manage this. However the patient by now was conscious, and although unable to speak because of the tube, indicated with his eyebrows that she could and should do it. The wife, clinical officers, and nurse, all rose splendidly to the occasion. After four days the tube was removed and later he went home healed.

Lack of equipment and 'making do' is still a continual feature of surgery. In 1894 raiders from Portuguese East Africa carried off all the surgical instruments in Mulanje Scots Mission, killing or wounding many villagers with gunshots. A man with a gangrenous arm arrived and they recorded: *as our surgical instruments have not yet been replaced, the amputating instrument was a pocket knife from Mr. Simpson; for dividing the bone we had a joiner's keyhole saw kindly lent by Mr. Moir.....the bone was cut through a little below the shoulder, and the stump is now healing nicely and he has quite given up the idea of dying.* Later Her Majesty's Commissioner donated £25 towards replacing these instruments carried off in the raid.

Today there are grave shortages of essential equipment in African hospitals. European and American charities sending containers full of medical supplies like rubber gloves, surgical dressings, catheters, sutures, and operating theatre equipment like sterilizers, provide most welcome aid which benefits thousands of suffering patients.

The early doctors in Africa built better than they knew. Their 'low tech' ideas are more appropriate today in the poor world than the 'high tech' ones often imposed by donors or aped by politicians in pursuit of 'excellence' - an awful word to the poor. One early mission hospital's spacious operating theatre had a roof window and the operating table could be moved to follow the shaft of bright tropical sunlight. At times, in differing hospitals I have had to move the operating theatre table near a window during the course of a proceedure because of light failure. In modern theatres, including some in Malawi, this would not be possible because there are only small lofty windows or none at all. Worse, when theatres are reliant on air conditioning and this fails, there are no windows to open.

There is a telling story of a 'state of the art' operating theatre block, built in the teaching hospital of a neighbouring country without windows that would open. The air conditioning units to fit into the ducts from the roof to the many theatres were not obtainable, so for some time the old theatres continued in use. Much later, when the new units arrived, the original donor government plans for the duct systems could not be found. The professor of surgery then had to go into the theatres and open an oxygen cylinder into each duct in turn while a colleague on the roof lit matches by the inlets to re-map the anatomy of the system.

Antiseptic surgery was carried out by the early doctors. Dr. John Kirk, Livingstone's companion in his Zambesi Expedition, was a fellow student at Edinburgh of Joseph Lister, the pioneer of antisepsis. Today most sterilizers and autoclaves (pressure sterilizers) are electrical, but when elements burn out they are expensive to replace. In many district hospitals the roar and heat of the primus stove underneath a simple autoclave is heard.

New technology can work provided there is money and expertise. It does work in one unexpected place in Malawi - at Embangweni Presbyterian Mission Hospital. It is reached by a twenty mile dirt road leading to it through a forest, and has no mains electricity. All the hospital's power comes from the sun, with a generator back up. Many

Solar Autoclave (sterilizer)

photovoltaic panels crown the ward roofs charging huge batteries which power the lights and X-ray machine. It also has one of the very few solar powered autoclaves in the world. A mobile array of glass tubes containing water/steam in a panel eight feet square is kept facing the sun in its path through the sky, by a solar powered motor. American mission money and expertise keeps it working. I always look forward to visiting this enthusiastic hospital. Mission hospitals are better supplied in many ways - often with one important asset, an expatriate maintenance engineer, which government hospitals usually lack.

The early doctors in Nyasaland all did some surgery but by the 1930s and '40s British doctors with extra surgical training were being sent out. They were pleasantly surprised by the lack of post-operative complications usually seen in Britain - pneumonia, wound infection, or deep vein thrombosis. The then accepted British practice was for post-operative patients to stay in bed for a week, now known to be a cause of complications. However their African surgical patients would not lie on their mats, but got up and walked around. Today this early mobilization is encouraged everywhere.

Before the AIDS epidemic, the lack of wound infection after operating in less than optimal sterile conditions was surprising. Perhaps it was because patients who came for routine surgery were survivors of the high infant mortality and of the bacterial and parasitic infections in their villages. They were often mentally and physically strong, thin and non-smokers. It has been suggested that some diseases of affluent people are due to life in too hygienic circumstances, they lack immunological challenge. A recent trial of giving short lived intestinal worms to patients with irritable bowel syndrome produced improvement.

Since the advent of the HIV-virus, operative wound infection has soared. Wounds may not heal by 'first intention' straight away but become infected, discharge pus, and break down before possibly healing. This happens even with the use of antibiotics. The early doctors would have expected wound infection, and be happy if it did not occur, as Dr. Prentice described in 1916:

We tackled the removal of what we knew to be a large abdominal tumour, and we soon found it to be a multilocular cyst and purulent at that (probably from the ovary). Jessie's mother sat beside the little path that leads from the operation room to the ward....to the poor old woman her daughter seemed dead. 'The maid is not dead but sleepeth' we said as we removed the covering blanket. Jessie's wounds healed by first intention, and she left the hospital completely cured.

Ovarian cysts still reach a huge size today before the patient comes for help. A thirty year old lady with her abdomen the size of a triplet pregnancy was driven to me by a clinical officer from a remote district hospital over appalling mud roads. He had to ford a fast flowing river because the bridge had been swept away. We operated together on her.

Through a relatively small incision, it was possible to suck out the contents (fluid and the cheesy like material and hair of a so called dermoid cyst) before removing it.

A protege of this Dr. Prentice mentioned above was Hastings Banda, who qualified as a doctor in USA in 1936. After practising in Britain and Ghana, he returned to Nyasaland in 1958 to lead the struggle for independence. However the first Nyasalander to qualify in medicine, also in the United States, was Dr. Malikebu who returned to reorganize Providence Industrial Mission in 1926.

Dr. S. Bhima was the first Malawian doctor to work in District Hospitals in 1952. Twelve years earlier he made his own way to Uganda by boats, lorries, and train, where he qualified at Makerere University. Subsequently specializing in Obstetrics and Gynaecology, he had to leave Malawi during the Banda regime. Happily at the end of the century he is working back in Blantyre again. But many Malawian doctors who left during the Banda era have not returned. Today increasing numbers of Malawian doctors are now undergoing specialist training. The challenge of the future will be the funding of the health and other services in a country so heavily reliant on foreign aid, and which is no longer able to feed itself.

Chapter 6.   Lake of Stars

"That great Lake Nyasa is so full of romance, so mixed up with everything African, dhows, Arabs, Coast men, travellers, missionaries, enterprises, traders, deaths, and treachery." - Dr. Wordsworth Poole 1896

Tales of Lake Nyasa spread to travellers across Africa for many decades before it was first sighted by David Livingstone, in 1859. Now called Lake Malawi, it lies at the southern end of the Rift Valley, its sparkling blue waters drained at the south by the Shire River flowing down to the River Zambesi. Three hundred and fifty miles long and fifty miles wide, the waters cover two thirds of the length of the country, forming the fourth largest and deepest freshwater lake in the world. Its waters make an as yet unspoilt paradise of nature, and the habitat for over five hundred species of unique mouth-breeding cichlid fish. Other smaller and shallow lakes like Malombe, Chiuta, and Chilwa, also form part of this Rift Valley water system.

We are now lucky to live for part of the year by this Lake and see its many moods and hear the water lapping on the shore as we go to sleep and awaken. For many years we would visit the Lake only at weekends.

Lake Malawi was maybe a cradle of mankind, for in 1992 a two and a half million year old jawbone of 'Homo Rudolphensis', an early hominid, was unearthed by archaeologists near Karonga. It is one of the oldest hominid bones ever found. Considering this jawbone, I began to wonder whether ancient Rudolph was able to catch fish for his family more easily than the overcrowded villagers living beside the lake of today?

Today, an ancient fishing way of life, which has sustained people along the shores of Lake Malawi for thousands of years, has become threatened by the rapid increase in the human population. Foreign donor policies both to improve income from fishing and to promote infant survival without birth control, caused a large lakeshore population increase after 1970. Foreign aided fisheries projects providing improved wooden boats, motor engines, trawling nets, and commercial facilities, resulted in huge catches of Chambo being sold in towns or exported.

During our many visits to the Lake we were embraced by the charm of the traditional fishing way of life. I wrote to our children:

Otters by Moonlight

"Along the lakeshore it was the zenith of the dry season, with leaves falling from the trees in showers, and clouds of smoke rising from grass fires on the distant mauve mountains. When we reached Cape Maclear, we sailed our plywood catamaran around Otter's Point to a small, lonely beach at dusk. During the night a total eclipse of the brilliant full moon occurred, just as it rose in a cleft of the high mountain behind us. It was spectacular to see the crescent shadow spreading across the moon, gradually darkening the quivering and luminous Lake waters until they became a mysterious inky black."

"Next morning we sailed to a very crowded village of about fifty small mud houses, where thatching was in full progress. Behind were the baobab trees, with their swollen trunks and twisted branches; pollinated by bats, the baobab flowers are said to be the home of bewitching spirits. The many wooden dugout canoes pulled up on the beach, the maize stores made of basket work, and the grass stockades fencing the houses, were a contrast to the brilliant blue waters of the Lake. Dozens of village men were out fishing in dugout canoes, each made from a whole tree trunk."

This scene changes as the moon wanes. In the shadows of the new moon, millions of lake flies called Kungu emerge from their larvae in the waters and arise in swirling brown clouds. Then, out in the deep waters of the Lake, shoals of small Usipa fish swim up to the surface waters to feed on these larvae.

By night, attracting these shoals to the shallow inshore waters is an ancient fishing operation. From our tent on the beach, under the crescent new moon, we saw many passing dugout canoes, carrying glowing brushwood flares or tilley lamps to attract the shoals towards their large encircling seine nets. There was activity and excitement throughout the night. The fishermen shouted to each other to signal the shoals, hitting the sides of their dugouts, and sometimes singing, harmonizing together across the water.

A meal of these little fish revived us once. A January storm had suddenly descended as we were sailing, whipping up the waves so we

Storms and Lake flies

could hardly turn our boat around. Thankfully we managed to avoid two hippos near a marsh ahead of us and steer into a little fishing village. The waves had been crashing over the platform of our catamaran and I was soaking and shivering in this wind.

The willing hands of kindly fishermen helped us pull our boat on the sand. On the beach, beside ochre yellow grass houses, thousands of tiny utaka and usipa fish were drying in the sun on reed tables. We bought some, and the headman kindly insisted we fry them in the pan on his fire and also boil some water for tea. We sat under a shady mango tree eating these little silver fish with our fingers - and with mango and a cup of tea it was delicious.

However, the most famous culinary delight of Lake Malawi is one of the many larger fish species, the big Chambo. It is a mouthbreeding fish - the fry shelter in the mother's mouth in times of danger, and it thrives in the shallow waters of the southern Lake and in the ajoining lakes of Malombe and Chilwa. Cookery books are full of gourmet recipes - chambo with lemons, with bananas, with garlic and groundnuts, or with cassava, with African sweet potatoes and tomatoes etc. It was calculated that by 1979, the chambo yield from the Lake was 22,000 metric tons, with fish then providing 70% of the animal protein in the nation's diet.

Already by then global foreign aid programmes were developing the lakeshore, the economic philosophy being 'give a man a fish and you supply one meal, but teach a man how to fish and you feed him for a lifetime,' (but perhaps 'fish out' the lake for his children). Boatyards were set up to construct plank fishing boats for use with outboard motors; and nylon nets were manufactured to replace the old large mesh nets traditionally made in the Lakeshore villages with fibre from the buaze plant. Modern fish marketing facilities with refrigeration were introduced in the programmes aided by benevolent foreign taxpayers; and boats together with more efficient nets ensured that some Malawian middlemen made money from bigger catches, which could be frozen and then transported to sell in towns. While the economy boomed and nets got bigger and better, the average human birthrate along the Lakeshore continued at eight babies per woman.

By the eighties, some of my university students first brought the news from their home villages that it was taking much longer to catch a fish in all the Lakes. Thirty years previously when herds of elephants could still be seen walking down through the indigenous forests along the shores to drink, and the entire human population of Nyasaland was only about two million (compared with about eleven million by 1999), a villager going out in a dugout canoe could apparently catch a fat fish for lunch within five minutes. Two generations later, his many grandsons have to paddle far out into the Lake and hold a line for twenty minutes before they have much luck with a bite.

Then in the nineties, a student reported the collapse of the chambo stocks in his own native Lake Malombe, linked to Lake Malawi:

The number of fishing boats on Lake Malombe has doubled in ten years, from about three hundred boats in 1980 to six hundred boats in 1990. With twice as many fishermen, it becomes more and more difficult to catch chambo. People are

Utaka and Usipa Fishing

now using mosquito nets to drag the waters, catching all the baby fish too. Fish yields have dropped to a tenth of what they used to be. The average fisherman now earns one tenth of the money he was making in the seventies and the ever increasing human population is a real threat to the survival of the chambo. In Lake Malombe, annual chambo catches fell from five thousand tons in 1980 to five hundred tons in 1990, (and to only one hundred tons by 1998).The root cause of all these problems is that there are now far too many fishermen. For the rapidly increasing numbers of youths, this is the only available livelihood. Some Lake Malombe fishermen have to move to Lake Chilwa, which is resented by Chilwa people, who are trying to keep out the Malombe men to preserve their own livelihood.

A Malombe community project has tried to transfer people from fishing and into agriculture and forestry. But the land is now so overcrowded that the agricultural department is trying to move young men off the land and into fishing. Trees have been cut down on the hills to the west of Malombe for people to open up vegetable gardens. This affects the heavy rains now running straight down the denuded hillside. Previously forests used to retain rainfall with the web of the tree roots acting like a sponge, which kept the perennial streams flowing down the mountain. But now the Malombe hillsides are bare and dusty with many disappeared brooks.

Most villagers live by fishing but catches are now far less than twenty years ago. The village land is also degrading because it can never be left fallow for one year now, as was the old custom, due to crop demand. Yields of maize are now far lower than they used to be. With deforestation, rainfall has decreased, and a huge dambo - a flooded area, can no longer be cultivated with rice. As the water table falls, two boreholes in the village dry up. Now that more people are drinking from, and bathing in, Lake Chilwa, diarrhoea and bilharzia have become more prevalent.

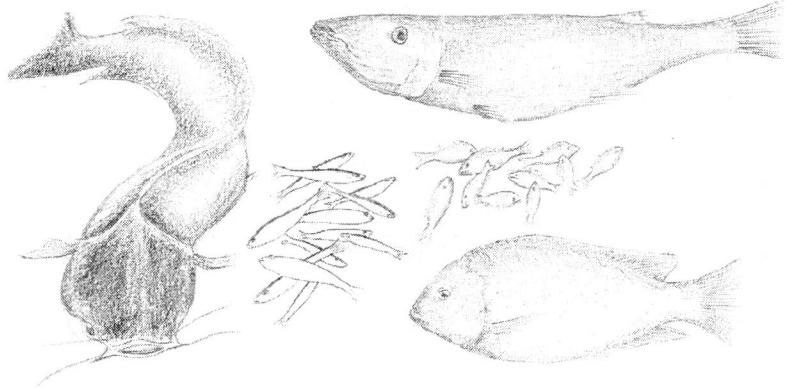

Foodfish, Mlamba, Usipa, Ncheni (top), Utaka, Chambo.

A village headman commented to me that the destitute are becoming ever poorer in this village. Polygamous wives and divorced women used to grow maize to sell to the fish sellers. Now they do not grow enough maize even to feed their own children, so increasingly they have had to turn to prostitution to earn money.

With many more mouths to feed in each family, there is less fish to sell, and increasing poverty and illiteracy. There is no family planning service around here.

So the increasing human population is necessarily leading to a decrease in fish stocks in Lake Malawi. Dr. Maurice King (no relation to us) first became internationally respected in the poor world for his writings on grassroots community medicine and his useful books for district hospital doctors. Now he has achieved more renown for his ideas on what is sustainable in poor countries, seeing clearly that over-population results in poverty, famine and strife. He stated that the more progressively a community is trapped in its population increase, the sooner it will starve.

The overfishing of Lake Malawi now probably forebodes more grave problems for the lakeshore people than the inhumanity of the old slave trade, which horrified David Livingstone and other British pioneers. After Queen Victoria established the British Protectorate of Nyasaland in 1890, by sending gunboats to Lake Nyasa to scuttle the Arab slave dhows, people could look to the future with optimism and even humour. Her Consul, Harry Johnston, managed to make a treaty with one notorious old Arab slave trader, the powerful Jumbe, at Nkhota Kota, and then raised the Union Jack to flutter over his lakeshore tribal domain.

So Queen Victoria decided to send Jumbe a personal diplomatic gift to grace this Chief's large Arab home overlooking the blue Lake waters. Harry Johnston recommended that a porcelain toilet service inscribed with 'V.R.I.' should be specially made in the Staffordshire potteries.

He later presented this extraordinary set to Chief Jumbe recording the unpacking at Nkhota Kota - *there was one awkward moment; in the array set forth on Jumbe's great verandah were two vessels not specially ordered by me, but supplied almost mechanically in those days with any complete toilet service. 'And what are these for?' said the delighted old man: and himself supplying the answer: 'I know! One for rice and one for curry!' And to that honourable function they were apportioned in the meal that followed.*

Nkhota Kota then became one of the first Anglican Mission stations. Here Bishop Chauncy Maples was buried in 1895, drowning after shipwreck. Storms whip up quickly and fishermen are sometimes drowned whilst out in dugout canoes. These heavy, unstable boats are very skilfully managed in the waves, boys even paddle them standing up. With fewer large, suitable trees remaining along the lakeshore, many are felled and made into boats inland, and rolled or transported by oxcart or lorry to the water. Some beaches may have forty or more canoes pulled up on them.

Making a dugout canoe

Over the years, Michael has designed and built several canoes. We spent our honeymoon in one, camping around bays in Southern Ireland. It was in a maiden voyage in another one, a plywood sailing canoe, that we had an encounter with a rogue baboon beside Lake Malawi, We were camping on a rocky headland, and Michael had paddled off around a nearby island. A large, solitary, male baboon came down and barked at me, and then rooted around in our tent pulling out the haversack, and examining each jar. Then he moved noisily towards me. I shouted and Michael paddled back quickly. The animal was unperturbed until he sized up Michael's height on landing, and made off - with our sugar.

We now keep our semi-rigid collapsible fibre-glass canoe on the beach by our tiny lakeshore home. It looks a little out of place among the other dugouts on the sand. We use it to go shopping and occasionally to visit the hospital, three bays away. Such a trip is always delightful. Silently we can float very close to birds and animals like the small Malachite kingfisher, the shy green backed heron, monitor lizards basking on the rocks, or young pythons curled up in the bushes overhanging the clear water.

Always we see the brilliant blue flashes of small mbuna fish among the rocks below us. Snorkling among them is like swimming among clouds of butterflies. Predominantly bright blue, but also with yellow, black and white markings, they are from one to four inches in size in a bewildering number of species and sub-species. Apparently they can change their colour and even sex. Feeding on the algae which covers the rocks like warm velvet, some make nests in the sand looking like minature, shallow volcanoes, which they defend against rivals.

Food fish are caught further out with long baited lines, or huge seine nets cast from dugouts and gathered up between canoes or on the beach. The catches must either be sold immediately because there is no refridgeration, or they are sundried or smoked on the beaches. They can then be packed into baskets or cardboard boxes and transported to inland towns to fetch higher prices. Your nose soon tells you if you are near a pickup truck full of dried fish.

Pied Kingfisher, Green backed heron, fish sand nests

For fifteen years we sailed a home-made catamaran bought in 1980 from a Scots engineer. One sunny, hot October morning, we set up the sails and launched into the heaving waters. In the strong southeast 'mvera' wind, we sailed eight miles straight across the Lake to the little uninhabited island of Boadzulu in forty minutes. Our boat was buffeted continuously by the crashing waves. Mooring off the northwest corner of Boadzulu in the lee of the wind, we collected twigs to make a campfire on the rocks and boil water for our morning coffee. The steep cliffs made landing difficult. Cormorants were continually arriving low over the north east horizon, flying in formation groups ranging from three to thirty birds. The trees and rocks were white with their droppings. They roost on Boadzulu in their thousands and rats feed on their fishy faeces.

Once we camped on this island and during the night two very poor fishermen from Mozambique arrived in a dugout, and asked if they could cook their fish on our fire. In tattered shirts, they huddled beside the flames all night. We managed to put up our tent on a little shelf of land and slept fitfully. Rats were scampering around and over us, through the night. One week later, I became very ill in Blantyre. Our physician diagnosed a form of typhus. He said I must have caught it from the fleas harboured by the Boadzulu rats. He had last seen a case like mine when he was imprisoned by the Japanese in Changi Jail at Singapore. I wondered whether those poor fishermen were sick too, and whether they could see a doctor and get tetracycline to cure it, as I did.

Another memorable night in camp was on a sand spit with a lagoon behind, with lightning flashing in all directions; we cooked our supper on a campfire. By 9 pm, half asleep in the tent, I heard a hippo grunting close by. I crawled outside, and during an extensive lightning flash right across the Lake, I felt the ground tremble and saw a huge hippo run straight by our tent down into the lake, at top speed, with a colossal splash. I never knew hippos could run so fast. We pulled our catamaran close in and slept nervously for the rest of the night, hearing other hippos grunting and splashing in the nearby waters.

The peaceful natural sounds of the Lake are rarely disturbed by motor boats. A few locally made plank boats with outboards are used to transfer villagers with katundu (luggage) from lakeside homes to towns. There are a few fishing and cargo ships, mainly in the south.

Some barges are used for bulk transport but the venerable 'Ilala' is the mainstay for passengers on her weekly voyage around the Lake. Built in Glasgow and reassembled on the Lake in 1951, she now has a smaller sister ship used when she is being repaired. Both are usually very overcrowded with passengers plus crates, rice, maize, planks of wood, iron sheets, chickens, and the inevitable dried fish in sacks. Third class passengers are crowded below decks on top of their belongings, there are a few cabins but second class passengers will sleep on deck, enchanting and cool at night under the stars - unless it is stormy or raining.

The 'Ilala' can only actually dock at two or three places, so at most of her dozen ports of call she has to anchor offshore after a warning blast on her hooter. She then lowers her two lifeboats and the scramble begins. Personal belongings and children are handed down into the rocking, rising and falling boat, and it motors on to the beach. There everyone jumps into the water as those wanting to board struggle to climb on.

The most most exciting dis- and em- barkations take place on the islands of Likoma and Chisumulu. This occurs at night with the Ilala's powerful searchlight playing on the beach as the only illumination if there is no moon. Hundreds wait on the beach, the deep shadows, the sound of the waves and the shouts of the boatman, the croaking of frogs, the smell, the good humoured excitement, it is all unforgettable.

The 'Ilala'

Chapter 7. Family Planning

"Ana ndi chuma cha mtosogola – Children are a wealth which can increase the number of mourners at funerals" Chewa proverb

Rich donor governments have assumed that people accept family planning as a way of living once they have health, wealth, and education. Quite likely the opposite is true. When men and women are able to make responsible decisions about marriage, and parenthood, then other benefits of modern living may be possible.

In our first post abroad in Malaysia in 1967, we saw the rapid improvement in the living standards of Singapore once the government had insisted citizens replace old fashioned Chinese concubinage with the one wife and two children policy. This was achieved with political and tax incentives and good family planning services. In that Chinese culture, the good of society took precedence over the rights of the individual.

I always remembered this example in the worsening poverty and polygamy of Africa. In our time in Swaziland, nurses whose royal husbands had taken more wives, were very bitter about this and one appeal of contraception is that it is a way to avoid polygamy; husbands have no need to take a second wife whilst the first is breastfeeding a baby, as the cultural norm required.

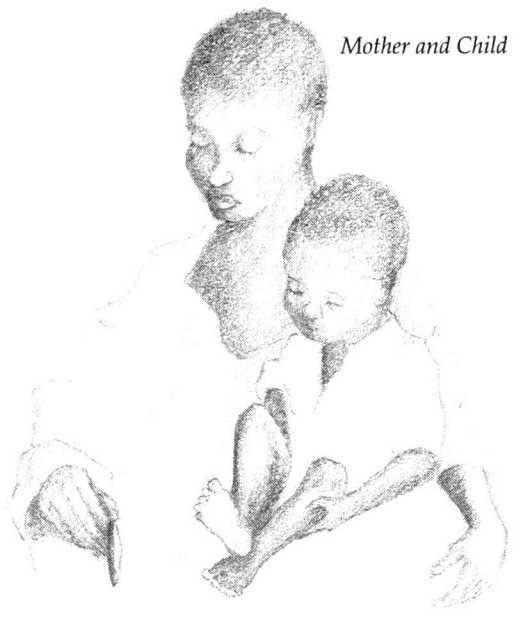
Mother and Child

Remarkably King Sobhuza approved of family planning services for his people in 1971, so the government asked me to give weekly lectures about birth control and marriage to the nurses. Today, almost thirty years later, that country has one of the best contraceptive prevalence rates in Africa. I used to publish my lectures in the local newspaper.

Then I had some amusing rows with polygamous Swazi Princes when I wrote that with birth control you only need one wife! This was read in the spirit in which it was delivered – gentle ribbing as opposed to inflammatory dialogue. This led me to conclude that everyone in the world basically would welcome access to modern contraceptives if given sufficient information and support, and that it was only Vatican-influenced agencies that would continue to be an impediment for many years.

UNICEF dodged this fundamental issue about contraception making monogamous marriage possible in African polygamous societies, through an oblique slogan 'when people see their children live they will want fewer.' The large number of mothers with more than ten living children in Malawi alone belied that claim.

As policies in African dictatorships are determined by one man, the personal situation of the ruler was important. Polygamist dictators of course warmed to UNICEF, as child-orientated policies implicitly supported both polygamy and high fertility. It also kept well paid UN officials in international jobs, although they had to speak carefully because they were only guests in African countries.

When President Banda came to power in 1964, he stopped all family planning in Malawi and told mothers to bear large numbers of babies to help their country, urging them that "We have no natural resources like gold here, our only wealth is people!"

Professional Malawians could see the urgent need for birth control, but they might have been in trouble if they had been too outspoken. It was less risky for expatriates to politick it. So Michael talked openly about contraception to hospital staff, and I gave lectures on the increasing population and birth control in Malawi.

We often discussed the problems over supper at home. Sadly the main method of birth control in Central Africa was, and perhaps still is, village abortion procured with cassava sticks. This is a major cause of maternal deaths. Michael was often called out to deal with the consequent peritonitis and septicaemia. This was an urgent humanitarian reason for modern contraception, in addition to the high infant mortality rate in families lacking food, and already burdened with too many children to feed and clothe.

After operating on President Banda's sister in 1979, Michael was well regarded, so after a Malawi Against Polio meeting at Sanjika Palace in 1980, he asked the official hostess if she would kindly see me about family planning. She agreed.

In the early December rains, I drove up though the summer gardens surrounding the modest but elegant Sanjika Palace with a sympathetic Malawian doctor's wife. Miss Cecilia Kadzamira and her sister Miss Mary came out to our car to welcome us and ushered us in to a private tea party. Servants carried in a silver tea service and beautiful china, and we nervously sipped tea and ate biscuits. This time I could not talk about marriage because these were single ladies. Cecilia was inevitably a feminist, because Kamuzu Banda had not married her; they were not reputed to be in love, so she had a strong and independent attitude to life. I would come to understand that African ladies in polygamous societies often feel humiliated and therefore bitter about men, especially in the matrilocal societies of south and central Malawi.

So I broached the topic circuitously – "Malawian women are terribly strained with continual childbearing. This is affecting their health. They are not able to achieve a human quality in their lives with this burden. I suffered much in pregnancy and childbirth, and I really feel sorry for mothers who have no escape from this continual ordeal. Family planning raises both the economic and personal status of women."

My friend elaborated on the health problems of high parity, to which Cecilia Kadzamira replied, "We are going to allow birth control here for women to space their pregnancies but it should be called child spacing. As you know, we do not have a population problem in Malawi and we have plenty of land up in the northern region here."

But this dangerous topic was not up for public debate or even general professional discussion, which meant that I wrote a few newspaper articles about contraception and romantic love and hoped for these hints to be taken up. My involvement continued at the inaugural meeting of the professional nurses' association in Blantyre in 1983. I organized an exhibition with Michael's posters about the dangers of rapid population increase, predicting food shortages. This had dire results.

We were summoned to fly to the Ministry in Lilongwe, accompanied by a nervous medical superintendent carrying the posters under his arm on the plane. The Minister of Health gave us a row, although sympathetic to the idea of contraception – the bottom line was that it was not politically correct to mention food shortages or population in Malawi. And I was told that I must stop writing newspaper articles and only speak in my Polytechnic lectures about this, telling Michael, "You must control your wife, in our culture the husband speaks, not the wife."

I was always aware that Malawians only listened to my ideas about family planning because I was the wife of a respected British surgeon. In the Polytechnic, my male students told me quite openly – "We enjoy having you as a lecturer because you are happy in your marriage. This is the kind of marriage we would prefer. It is better than the strife in our village polygamy." Because of this matrimonial asset, and my Ph.D. degree, I was locally employed by the University of Malawi for fourteen years and given every encouragement to teach the issues about exponential growth of population, marriage customs, and birth control. It was rewarding work with an enthusiastic response from the undergraduates.

Malawian students were more explicit about family planning taboos. The average African male resists contraception and all the feminist propaganda that goes with it, because he feels threatened by losing his authority in his matrimonial relationship. When a couple have not united for love, continual pregnancies are needed to bond the marriage.

I was told that most men disliked and even feared the long succession of independent, freelance, foreign women arriving to spearhead birth control programmes. And as they watched these powerful ladies, husbands thought – 'We Malawians do not want our women to become like that' and concurred that 'I will have no control over my wife once she has contraceptives.'

Sometimes we met the kind of Europeans they feared. We were invited to an American feminist party. The mysterious beauty of the African night with brilliant stars and moonlight, softly calling owls and night-jars, and singing ciccadas, was suddenly drowned by the harsh, deep, competitive, voices of a dozen ambitious female doctors with short cropped hair, clad in workaholic trousers and battle shirts. Some were struggling through their twelfth academic year at Harvard, and spent much time pushing research 'facts' into computers.

I feared privately that their preconceived and overwhelming attitudes about female empowerment would result in bogus research – gender equality theories seem to dehumanize feminine instincts, and may pervert perception of the real needs of both children and African women. A nun who had jumped over the convent wall was saying "if men menstruated, we should have a different kind of world."

It is interesting that the message about the positive marriage relationship made possible with contraception is a winner in Malawi. This was originally offered by Marie Stopes when she pioneered birth control in Britain during the twenties. In 1992 this proved very popular when first presented in a 'Man to Man' propaganda programme by the Banja la

Mtosogola organization in Malawi, which resulted in British aid giving the project a lot of financial support.

Sadly though, going back to our meeting with the Malawian Minister of Health back in 1983 – three weeks after seeing us, he was horribly murdered, with three other politicians. A judicial enquiry, twelve years later, stated that the four gentlemen were bludgeoned to death by police "acting on higher instructions". The bodies were dumped in an overturned car at Mwanza on the Mozambique frontier road.

For another long decade, the considerable foreign donor support for the Banda regime, meant little progress in family planning in Malawi. The service was available but a very few women took the Pill. Western donors did not perceive the real difficulty which was frequently brought to my notice by students. Quite simply the problem was the old African culture where people did not marry for love, with different attitudes prevailing in varying tribal traditions.

Students from the southern matrilocal tribes wrote: *In Chewa tribal customs, the husband proves his virility by procreation; so Chewa wives think that once they are pregnant, they can demand anything they want from their husbands or relatives.*

And the Northerners identified these other norms of their patrilocal tribal traditions: *The Ngoni husband has total control of the sexual performances, and he wants to beget as many children as possible.* So without romance, continuous procreativity is a social reality that forces women into an emotional desert.

Women students also told me more about the Malawian woman's status: *If a lady does not become pregnant soon after marriage, she becomes the target of village gossip suggesting she has got bad diseases or is bewitched with evil spirits. She is despised and her husband must take a second wife. In all cases women are victims of the African situation. A baby is the axis on which her life depends, as it is the baby that secures her marriage. A man has to take a second wife if the first one does not bear him a son. Underneath our men still believe in what their grandfathers taught them. Other women report having many babies to reduce the chances of their husbands leaving them.* So a high birthrate in poor Africa is self perpetuating because it keeps these people poor, ignorant, hungry, and also drives them into old sorcery fears.

This coercive polygamous culture has had sad environmental consequence: in 1985 a student studied the large families in his village beside Lake Chilwa. *When my father first arrived here twenty-five years ago, the grass grew about two metres high and was deep green. Now it only grows to half that height and is turning yellow. We now see many 'chindalala', that is barren strips of land. In the downward spiral of this poverty trap, people lose their food and farming security, and their whole traditional family life begins to break up, men go away to find work, many mothers have to resort to prostitution for money, and children grow up in this overcrowded and worsening situation.*

In my own village there is now a tragic increase in quarrelling, jealousy, and witchcraft. As I am writing now, a witch doctor, the 'halawalawa' has been called in to investigate and uncover all witches and wizards. Some witches have already been indicated, others, their witchcraft powers removed, have been sternly warned to stop their evil practices or they risk death.

It is a terrible tragedy that these villagers have not been helped to see that their problems are due entirely to the rapid population increase. Before we defend a person's human right to beget children, have we considered the tragic psychological consequences of an ever increasing population in this world?

As usual, I had to hide the explosive words of this essay in the wardrobe, or the student might have been in danger.

Many other contradictory tribal notions about marriage and procreation could be heard from my students, all with one common feature of fear in matrimonial relationships. *An African husband regards childbearing as a means of keeping his wife under control. Women fear that if they use contraceptives, they will be divorced and have no money to look after their children. Men should be the main target of family planning propaganda, because they make sexual decisions in our culture.*

The Yao and Lomwe tribes have primitive teachings about procreative sex in their initiation ceremonies at puberty; these initiation customs could be reformed to give modern contraceptive education instead. If everyone had the feeling that it would be better to beget one professor than ten thieves, birth control might be acceptable.

Methods of birth control also need sympathetic consideration in Africa. At first there was not a large uptake of the contraceptive pill in Malawi. In the early eighties, our hospital matrons told me there was an urgent need for more units of the injectable drug 'depo-provera', a contraceptive doubted in Europe because it diminishes menstruation.

However poor malnourished African mothers seem to prefer to lose less monthly blood for both health and cultural reasons, and much prefer injections to pills; one very beneficial feature of depo-provera is that it maintains lactation in breast-feeding mothers. It is the ideal contraceptive to reduce distressing infant malnutrition rates.

However when I teleponed some of the aid donors in Lilongwe, the response was negative. They were advised by experts at home. Only the German ambassador was positive. Within a week she arrived at our kitchen door bearing many boxes of this drug, as urgently requested, because so many mothers at the hospital were asking for it.

Today this contraceptive is still wanted by 98% of the mothers at rural clinics in Malawi. Unfortunately this depo-provera injection protects a mother from pregnancy for only three months, and in the tropical storms of Central Africa she may have problems coming back across flooded roads for the next injection, or at times when she is busy with planting or harvesting crops. In Malawi, August is the best season for a poor woman to make the long journey to the health centre, so an implant that would protect her for a single year might be ideal.

Sadly, because depo-provera was not approved by the Food and Drug Administration in the United States until 1996, American family planning programmes in Malawi were not able to offer it for sixteen years. So, the Blantyre contraceptive prevalence rate remained at about 2% for a long time.

Many Malawian women have asked for Norplant – a similar progesterone implant that protects against pregnancy for five years. Again, international politicking has made supplies of this useful drug difficult to obtain.

However sorcery pressures for high fertility are still flourishing in Malawi, even in the cities. One humid January afternoon, with looming heavy black clouds behind the striking scarlet flowers of the flame of the forest trees, Michael and I were walking around Blantye's Soche mountain. A thuderstorm suddenly enveloped us, with battering rains and fearsome lightning flashes creating an atmosphere of supernatural powers and sorcery. A witch doctor kindly invited us to take shelter in his dark little mud and thatched home, adorned with pictures of Christ with owl's wings. He brought out 'nsupe' pots of his medicine to cure female infertility, and told us nearly all his many patients, both male and female, came complaining of their failure to procreate! This was the major worry all around Blantyre.

The high birthrate is the real problem of Central Africa. If suffering on a colossal scale is now to be prevented, then foreign aid to poor African countries should not just carry conditions of democracy, but a humanitarian demographic conditionality is also required. When I published national newspaper articles on this theme in 1992, there was not a single objection from thousands of Malawian readers to my weekly advice about 'one wife and two children'.

It could be argued that if poor and uneducated people are coerced by witchcraft traditions, then there is also a moral case for strong support to help them out of this culture trap to live responsibly in the modern world. This is the ethical issue which should be faced by both rich donor governments and African governments.

One very hopeful feature of the Malawian tribal societies is their communal village cohesion and alleigance to the chiefs. Students told me a monogamous marriage and population policy could be happily effected if the paramount chiefs were to discuss these problems with the village men, and male family decisions are what matter in Africa.

Donors have presumed gender programmes would reduced high birthrates. But by 2000 gender policies too have not succeeded in Malawi. A free primary school education programme strongly supported by British aid funding has seen girls' literacy rates dropping gravely below the previous 40% in 1994 to an estimated 25%. Sick, malnourished children from families struggling to survive in an overpopulated land cannot easily learn.

In spite of free secondary schooling for girls financed by USAID the Malawian Secondary Certificate of Education pass rate has declined each year from 73% in 1994, to 13% in 1999. When sometimes only 2% of secondary school leavers have the hope of finding a job or course of training in overpopulated Malawi, there is not much incentive to learn. A lower birthrate is necessary for improved education.

To the Initiation Ceremony, Charcoal and Wood for sale

Chapter 8.   Sanjika Palace

Elderly President Banda began his long reign in Malawi with high hopes for progress, which were sadly defeated by the rapidly increasing human population needing ever more food and firewood. Well into old age, he was trying to prop up the old African polygamous society with its high birthrate, by soliciting foreign aid. Inevitably this ever worsening poverty led to social unrest, which could only be thwarted with severe political intimidation by the government. As worldwide belief in 'African development' became like a religious dogma, so perhaps the rich governments should be blamed too for the consequent human rights abuses and strife. Worse still, this global expectation has also caused the Malawi government to build schools, roads, hostels, clinics, airports, palaces, etc with borrowed money, which has resulted today in Malawi being indebted to the World Bank agencies for no less than two billion US dollars.

Lasting reform can only come from ideas and action within a society, so Michael and I felt that we could only work if we spoke out about both the prison abuses and the human population problems.

Kamuzu Banda's early achievements were impressive; after attending a mission school under a fig (kachere) tree , he travelled to South Africa and eventually made his way to the United States, qualifying as a doctor in 1937. After a year at Edinburgh in Scotland, he practised in Liverpool and North London, departing to Ghana in 1953. He returned to Nyasaland in 1958 to lead the political struggle for independence, becoming the President of Malawi at the age of sixty six, to rule with absolute power for thirty years 1964-94.

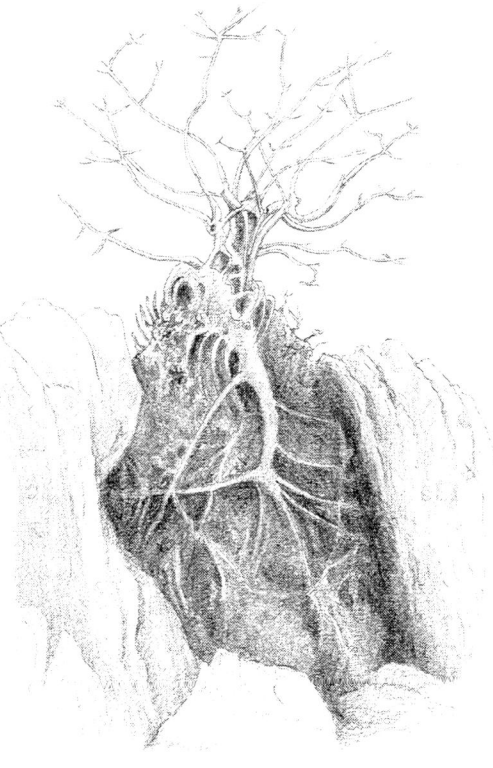

One of the varieties of Kachere tree; a Strangler Fig

However this President lived in a rather lonely state, far removed from the increasing poverty of his people. The modest houses built for British governors of Nyasaland were not enough for this dictator. He ended up with abodes like the British sovereign, moving in style from one to another. Many people were worried at the huge expenditure on his new palace at Lilongwe, which he never occupied. His favourite residence was in Blantyre, Sanjika palace on the top of a hill, with a view across the blue hills to the Great Rift Valley, to which we were occasionally invited on public occasions. I always went in nervously, since I had criticized the tortures in prisons in the Polytechnic.

The hospital mortuary was receiving horrid corpses from prisons and I was soon to see the living reality. Driving along an avenue of flaming poinsettia trees on one winter morning in 1984, passing a prisoner looking like a Belsen victim, I stopped and asked the guards if I could take him to hospital. He had collapsed into the ditch and was obviously starving, with limbs denuded of muscles, shiny wrinkling skin, and thin hair crawling with lice. Warders were escorting him to the traditional court for his murder trial. They agreed, and they all stepped into our van, and off we went.

I spent the whole morning negotiating with the police before eventually driving right into the prison to get permission from the governor; the gates were locked behind us and I began to feel the terror of someone who matters less than a starving dog, upon hearing that eight hundred men and forty women were crowded into this little old colonial prison. Staff said there was not even room for the convicts to lie down at night, and they had to sleep sitting up back to back in a hall called the 'shamba'. Permission was finally given for me to take our collapsing prisoner to the QE hospital, but there he was spirited away when unguarded on his way from outpatients to the ward - and was never seen again.

Thankfully I went home to lunch, finding Michael had come back with an invitation to the Independence day state banquet at Sanjika palace. It would be a great contrast to the tragic misery I had just seen. In this sunny winter season, I washed my frilly white ball dress, and brushed the mould off Michael's dinner suit, made by a Hong Kong street tailor thirty years ago when he was in the Royal Artillery. It still looked quite smart. So we drove up to Sanjika palace in our party clothes.

The previous year we declined a palace invitation after four government ministers had been killed in 'a car accident' - battered to death with hoes on official orders. In the small palace entrance hall furnished with Louis XV chairs, I drank a glass of sherry to sustain me through the evening ahead. I knew the place was full of political spies, it was not safe to make open comments; any Malawian overheard talking about food shortages was in trouble, and might end up in the prison conditions I had seen. This palace had a treacherous atmosphere like a mediaeval castle, so I had to talk about dresses and flowers.

Then we went into the banqueting hall. The Miss Kadzamiras, as official hostesses, were always able to provide charming receptions. At each long table, delicately set with china, silver cutlery, and cut glass, were ladies on one side and men the other. Whilst the army band played popular tunes, Michael commented on the Battle of Waterloo as he ate Beef Wellington, sitting between the French ambassador and one of the university principals. The latter was nice enough to tell Michael that I did my academic job well.

I was placed next to a judge's wife, and opposite the chief of Lilongwe police, a man in charge of the infamous political special investigation branch. I tried to keep chatting for a long three hours about gardens, sailing, and birth control. Nearby was the Charge d'Affairs from Mozambique, who assured me his country was a marvellous place for a holiday if tourists travel everywhere by air. None of the roads were safe, because people were shot up by bandits.

The following night we briefly attended the Independence ball. Michael and I danced together to a very good band with a soloist singing
"If I say you've got a beautiful body, Will you hold it against me?"

Social life continued. A month afterwards we dined at the Royal College of Surgeons of Edinburgh and learned that President Banda had donated many thousands of pounds towards building a hostel for foreign doctors studying in Edinburgh. The British government allowed the Malawian doctors given training in UK to remain in Britain. They could not have been unaware of the thousands of poor Africans suffering and dying back home in Malawi without their own doctors. The leadership of a numerous and dynamic Malawian medical profession was also needed to sort out the nation's birth control problems and give the public advice which would be respected. But very few Malawian doctors ever returned home from Britain.

Meanwhile back in our Queen Elizabeth hospital at Blantyre, a hostel originally built for twenty Rhodesian nurses was now the crowded home of nearly a hundred student male medical assistants, who took it in turns to sleep in the bedrooms by day or by night. After walking the crowded wards and clinics all day, these boys had only eight chairs to sit on at lunch. I had recently held a jumble sale to raise money to buy more benches for them. I told the Edinburgh surgeons I was disappointed and angry with their university for taking this money, when it should have been spent on Malawian students training at home who would stay in their own country to care for so many sick and suffering people.

Another year an invitation came for a midday reception on the palace lawns; we wrote to our daughters:

"May 5th 1985, we are going to President Banda's birthday party at Sanjika palace. I shall wear the regency style muslin dress I bought in Brighton, and I am getting out that pink nylon hat that I last wore in Turkey on our overland journey to Malawi. I have put two roses over the stain on the band, and if I wash the whole hat, it should look quite fresh - Mum."

"May 9th, we have the Sanjika party next Tuesday, which is usually an interesting affair in a lovely garden on the hilltop with a terrific view, the band playing, and Mummy making 'contacts' in her pink hat - Dad."

"May 16th, our palace garden party ended in pouring rain and a chiperoni mist descended on the mountain, so much so that the foreign ambassadors and local politicians could hardly be seen - not to mention the waiters carrying around delicious finger food on silver trays.

In such cold weather, I had decided to wear my own Campbell of Cawdor tartan which was very appropriate for the Macbeth atmosphere up at the palace. The guests began to look like smokey apparitions in these swirling clouds, becoming visible, and then fading away across the lawn. I wondered whether some of them were the ghosts of political opponents who have been 'fed to the crocodiles.' - Mum."

On the palace lawns, we met lots of people sipping iced drinks at this birthday party. The British High Commissioner with his wife dressed in powder blue, greeted us warmly, and we talked to an American mission surgeon and his wife about our next concert - as music and art are taught instead of sport at Adventist schools, they were superb players of the piano and flute.

Then the French ambassador told us that of a hundred French people in Malawi, about thirty were Catholic priests, either Montfort Fathers in the south or the redoubtable White Fathers in the northern and central areas.

Two Malawian doctors were very enthusiastic about our family planning politicking, but they soon departed to Britain for further training and never returned to Malawi.

The army band played, and the official hostess, Cecilia Kadzamira, looking gracious in a brilliant green ankle length silk outfit, ushered the elderly President to the dais. She was twice his height and half his age and had devoted her life to caring for this man, then nearly ninety years old. They received each ambassador in turn. Rumours abounded that the hostess' family held the reins of power. But there was one difference from mediaeval Europe - much power in south Malawi was based on female solidarity.

Typically, they paid special attention to the only female diplomat, the German ambassador who wore a Bohemian style hunting hat with a bush shirt dress, all in pheasant brown. Another militant feminist, the American army attache's wife, wore Malawi Womens' League uniform, the chirundu - a cotton sheet around her hips, with Kamuzu Banda's smiling face draped across her buttocks.

Also attired in chirundus were dozens of the President's womens' league ladies sitting, in charming village style, in groups on the lawn. They were the polygamous 'Chikamwini wives' whose husbands floated in and out of their homes and lives like waves on a seashore. Sadly they ended up with no husband to take them to parties.

However one Malawian lady with a very powerful politician husband approached me cheerfully to discuss her efforts with a slimming diet. She loved food and once did a catering course in Europe. I dared not tell her that a week in a notorious government prison would do the trick beautifully.

Hastings Kamuzu Banda's age was a mystery. Officially he was born on May 14 1906. Strange rumours circulated secretly though about his origin, and some political critics called him the 'hybrid chicken'. His mother was a Kasungu girl of Chief Mwase's Chewa clan, who conceived after she was given herbal roots by the witch doctor to cure infertility. Kamuzu means 'little root' and Hastings was the surname of a Scots missionary.

One Malawian opposition politician told me this intriguing tale: "I was at Blantyre airport in July 1958, when Dr. Hastings Banda made his famous return to Nyasaland, after forty three years away in America, Britain, and Ghana. His presumed relatives from Kasungu had gathered to welcome their long lost son as he stepped off the aeroplane. As the journalists were surrounding his old great uncle, Reverend Hannock Phiri of Kasungu, they asked whether he remembered Kamuzu as a child, and in what year he was born?

Prison Van

'Kamuzu was born in the year of the famous locust plague at Kasungu - that was in 1898' replied the uncle. Dr. Banda then looked around nervously and told his aides 'Shut up that old man', because his passport gave his year of birth as 1906! Old Uncle Hannock Phiri then commented that Hastings Banda did not even speak the local Chewa dialect of Kasungu, and so wondered whether he was genuine, or, like a mediaeval prince, possibly even a changeling?"

A few years afterwards, the greatly respected Kasungu Chief Mwase was publicly denounced by President Banda, and then beaten up, because he had asked if a rebel Malawian could please be reconciled to the government. The ancient chieftainship of the Kasungu Chewa tribe, Kamuzu's mother's clan, was then abolished. The Chewa tribal people were greatly shocked by this.

One of my students told me President Banda's political power base spread like an octopus from the palace into every sphere of life - the following tale from a Dutch doctor highlighted it: a local party politician kept walking into his district hospital to spy on everybody and everything going on. The Dutchman became annoyed at the way he commandeered staff facilities, and asked him please not to use the staff toilet. A week later this doctor was sacked from his job by the Malawi congress party and ordered to go to Lilongwe - he had been actually dismissed from the loo!

In 1989, the Silver Jubilee year of Malawi's Independence, the British Prime Minister, Mrs.Thatcher arrived, one of the trinity of famous foreign visitors; the other two were the Archbishop of Canterbury and the Pope. Distress was increasing, with floods, famine, and pestilence abounding. Even the BBC was at last broadcasting serious worry about the large number of inmates suffering in Malawian prisons, with many dying. Amnesty International had even given a dossier about this to Mrs. Thatcher. Until now the motto for foreign donors had been nothing like 'an eye for an eye and a tooth for a tooth', but instead seemed to be 'give big rewards of British taxpayers' money to regimes practising widespread abuses of human rights.' But nobody was very keen to listen to our protests, not even the United Nations agencies.

Despite our beliefs, we could not refuse a state event to honour our British Prime Minister. On the big day, Blantyre was en fete by dusk, with hundreds of fluttering Union Jacks and crowds of singing and dancing womens' league ladies lining the streets. It was a female power festival! I saw Mrs. Thatcher in brilliant green waving to them from her car.

Michael and I were invited to the State Banquet in her honour at Sanjika Palace. We set off with heavy hearts again for the thousands of suffering prisoners in Malawi, including a Malawian surgeon recently arrested for his policy disagreement with the President. Michael was the only British doctor at this banquet, the other Britons were businessmen.

Mrs. Thatcher arrived in a pale mauve tweedy looking dress, with low square neck, pearls, and one diamond clasp. President Banda who always felt safer with women, looked on full of pleasure as he chatted. At over ninety, he was probably not the most exciting politician she had met, but she buttered him up most of the time and he obviously liked her attention. Even though I resented her comparing Kamuzu Banda to David Livingstone in her speech, Mrs. Thatcher outshone everyone that night, and, sitting with the silver and porcelain at the high table, she reminded me of a wax figure, often moving into the chamber of horrors at Madame Tussauds.

As we walked down to the car park after midnight, under bright stars, looking across to the Great Rift Valley, the fiction about Malawian development expressed in the official speeches, seemed sad. It could not be known that far deeper problems were hidden from European politicians, and foreign hopes for rural improvement could not flower in the witchcraft that dominated the villages in this vast landscape.

I had written in my diary that day: "Only ten miles away from Blantyre at Madziabango Village, on the main tar road to Chikwawa, there is now a lot of evil witchcraft going on. A medical assistant has been murdered in sorcery rituals because the villagers feared he caused some deaths with evil magic, and so the government health centre has had to close. Medical assistants with protection now visit this village only by day. So witchcraft wins against progress again."

In African culture, people escape from unacceptable reality by putting on masks for sorcery ceremonies with dancing. Our escape from the fictional foreign 'development' politics next day was to climb up the steep Likulesi path to the plateau of Mulanje, the highest mountain in Central Africa. Abruptly rising 6,000 feet to the plateau and then to 9,000 feet at the summit, Mulanje towers over the Phalombe plains like an vast, impregnable, granite fortress. I wrote in my diary

"The day is clear and we have a wonderful view of Lake Chilwa. Scattered across the sweet smelling braken and grass on the plateau are dozens of proteas, red flowering aloes in rocky clefts, Mulanje buttercups, wild pink and mauve gladioli, and many orchids. Very wearily, after four hours of climbing, we reach Thuchilla forestry hut and boil water from the mountain stream to make our welcome cup of tea.

We cook our supper over the scented Mulanje cedar logs in the glowing fire. Then at dusk, dynamic thunderstorms coming in from the Indian Ocean envelope the mountain, with hissing rain and roaring thunderclaps re-echoing around the peaks. Last night we witnessed the politicking of sad delusions, but tonight we sit with more realism on the floor of an isolated African mountain hut beside the dying embers of the fire."

Next morning huge volumes of water were pouring off the mountain, and in crossing the Likulesi we had to slide down a steep rock in the rushing stream, grimly holding on to tufts of grass. As we departed, colossal waterfalls were pouring off Mulanje Mountain - ensuring our respect for the overwhelming powers of nature.

Two days later I heard more about Mrs. Thatcher's visit when our Anglican priest called for tea. He had just conducted the funeral of a member of Ndirande township Mothers' Union, a vegetable seller in Ndirande market; having not cleared up her stall and money in time to go to cheer Mrs. Thatcher with the womens' league in Blantyre last Wednesday, the Presidential youth league had started beating her up, and she died. She was buried in the Anglican churchyard on Sunday. And the priest informed us that no one was arrested for this. A quotation from Shakespeare's Scottish play Macbeth came to mind:

> *"Now I think you can behold such sights*
> *And keep the natural ruby of your cheeks."*
> *When mine is blanched with fear."*

Chapter 9. The Grim AIDS Reaper

*"We are the Dead. Short days ago
We lived, felt dawn, saw sunset glow,
Loved and were loved." – John McCrae 1918*

By 1996 the World Bank reported *"The HIV epidemic in Malawi is one of the most severe in Africa and in the world and there are no indications that the incidence of new infections has been slowed."* The expenditure of international taxpayers' money on preventing the disease with health education had failed, whilst there was little possibility in providing care for the ever increasing numbers of people dying in hospitals. The emphasis on preventive medicine instead of curative services by the European Union and American donors was to the detriment of African hospitals in the 1990s, when they were faced with human suffering on an unprecedented scale.

By 1999, over one million people are feared to be infected with the HIV-virus in Malawi, and an estimated 250,000 patients are dying each year from this disease. However demographers have predicted that AIDS will not diminish the population problem in Malawi, but will only reduce the annual rate of population increase from 3.5% to 2.2%. But such predictions can be wrong.

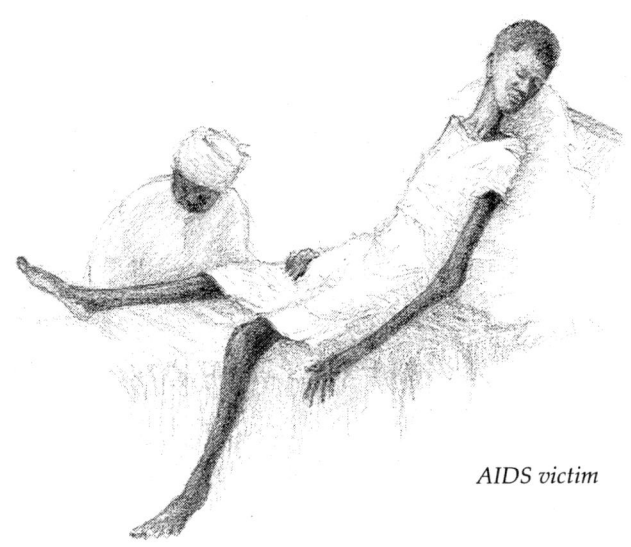

AIDS victim

At an East African Surgeons conference in 1992 it was noted that women are biologically more vulnerable to the HIV-virus. They catch it at a younger age and the disease progresses in females more quickly, with a resulting earlier death. More drastically, a gender imbalance in East Africa was predicted within a decade, with men outnumbering women perhaps by three to two.

In the nineties, some social patterns in this disease have been defined. Rural hospital staff commented that two categories of people are at much higher risk of HIV-infection, namely polygamous spouses in the villages and educated urban people. An analysis of statistics at Queen Elizabeth Hospital in Blantyre city, has indicated that a woman whose husband has attended more than eight years at school is twice more likely to be HIV-positive than a poor peasant woman. And ladies whose husbands are peasant farmers have significantly lower HIV-prevalence rates than those whose partners are either professionals, skilled workers, or in the army or police.

Similar high rates of AIDS infection are found in skilled and professional women themselves, who are three times more likely than the wives of peasants to be HIV-positive. So the protagonists of education as the remedy to Africa's problems may have to think again. The marriage stakes may even change! An illiterate spouse could soon be a more desirable match. These statistics are perhaps paralleled in a British survey showing higher levels of promiscuity amongst the best educated Britons.

During the summer storms, when heavy clouds darkened the mountains of north Malawi, and lightning flashes cracked the skies, Ngoni and Tumbuka medical assistants pointed out that traditional polygamists are a high HIV risk group, which highlights the fatal nature of polygamy. Sadly it is not based on loving and faithful unions. Wives, and maybe their husband, sneak off to other liasons. We were told of eight HIV deaths in nine weeks in one such family, – parents, grandfather, aunt, uncle, daughters and a son all sickened and perished – all these funerals within two months.

Some European and Asian patients presented in Malawi. For instance, a British man with persistent rectal bleeding, had been investigated in a London hospital, without a cause being found. He returned to a hospital in Malawi. It seemed a strange medical problem, until his painted girl friend sat down beside his bed in the ward. The suspicious doctor then found his AIDS-test was positive.

Another Portuguese engineer who left his wife and baby at home whilst he came to work on a contract, said on finding he was HIV-positive: "I cannot go home now, if I stay here at least my child will have one parent." Many Peace Corps volunteers and VSOs went home with HIV even though stern warnings had been given beforehand.

In Blantyre, increasing numbers of civil servants, university professors and lecturers who were my colleagues, hospital staff, lawyers, teachers, businesss staff, engineers, and accountants, were dying of AIDS. Everywhere, across the social spectrum, vital skilled people were disappearing – a mechanic, a technician, a printer, a salesman, a secretary, a clerk.

The World Bank reported *AIDS is affecting a higher than proportionate number of skilled and educated people – one company reported a sixfold increase in mortality between 1991 and 1995. The epidemic is predicted to have a significant impact on economic development, slowing GDP growth by 1.5% annually. There will be significant loss of aggregate earnings resulting in increased poverty. Sectors whose profits are reliant on mobile, educated, young, and urban, workers will be more affected economically.*

Furthermore, the result of this disease in the countryside was a rapidly growing number of child headed families, who, because of their youth and burdened life, farmed their gardens less efficiently. Many services were affected by loss of skills.

At one lakeshore hospital, where the people came in dugout canoes past the calling fish eagles and landed beside the shady mango trees, a trained radiography technician was dying of HIV. As a final gesture, he taught the hospital tailor how to take X-Rays. The latter did the job quite well for a year, before he too collapsed with AIDS. However before his demise, he passed on these skills to a gardener, whose pictures were not so good; but for a while this did not matter because the hospital then ran out of cash to buy more X-ray films.

Back in the cool highlands at Blantyre, I was asked to visit one of my former Polytechnic students, Stanley, who had been ill in hospital for nine weeks and was not recovering. No one would tell his young wife Wezi what was wrong, she could not understand why he could not get better. She was eight months pregnant and had been a virgin when she married him the previous year.

Three days later Stanley died, and a notice appeared in the newspaper a month afterwards: "Stanley, I still can't believe you are dead. The gap you left will never be filled. It is sad you did not wait for your first born child, Stanley Jnr. to be born. Wife Wezi and Stanley Jnr."

Then junior sickened with wasting and skin ulcers and died within four months. And so Wezi began her final suffering illness with Kaposi's Sarcoma and died a year afterwards. The tragic fate of this young family was typical of thousands.

In the bungalow style wards of the Queen Elizabeth hospital, where patients go out to sit beside flowering shrubs in the morning sunshine, a

Malawian clinician despaired about the epidemic in 1994: "Three quarters of our hospital patients now have AIDS. I cannot understand why society is not waking up to do something about this disease. When I tell relatives a patient has HIV, they usually refuse to believe it. Only yesterday parents claimed their two sons had died of malaria when they know it was AIDS."

This social denial has spread far beyond the local community. For the first ten years of the epidemic, civil servants, diplomats, rich donor governments, and UN agencies, were behaving like ostriches with their heads in the sand about AIDS in Africa. International financial support to promote safe promiscuity certainly took precedence over action for the suffering and dying.

Inappropriate policies for Africa have been formulated partly because different strains of AIDS may prevail in Europe and America. In Britain in the year 2000, it is reported *Over 70% of AIDS cases have been reported in homo- or bi-sexual men. Sex between men and women is the mode of infection in almost a third of new cases of HIV infection in the United Kingdom. Most of these infections have been acquired abroad – primarily in sub-Saharan Africa.* Europe has not yet experienced the flowering of this heterosexually transmitted HIV-1E virus prevalent in Central Africa. But AIDS has no definite boundaries, no strict preferences.

At afternoon tea in our garden in 1992, as the Heughlings Robin was singing melodiously under the flame of the forest tree at dusk, an Edinburgh physician told us that about 90% of TB patients in Malawi were by then infected with the HIV virus. Michael noted that a huge increase of pulmonary TB was linked with AIDS, but the incidence of bone TB and intestinal TB remained little changed.

Interestingly, leprosy did not proliferate with HIV-infection, although the TB and leprosy bacteria are similar. In fact the opposite happened; as leprosy was dying out in the ten years 1985-95, helped by the drug treatment programme organized by a British charity LEPRA. When people become infected with HIV they die of something else first because leprosy is such a slow disease. The leprosy bacillus takes eleven days to multiply, whereas a TB germ only takes ten hours.

African culture is not easily understood by outsiders. One Malawian medical student commented that on returning to his village in 1993, he found many of his former friends had died of HIV. They had a reckless attitude to AIDS because the local poverty, coupled with unloving polygamous traditions, offered little motivation in this life.

Our cook reiterated that most villagers thought AIDS is a disease caused by witchcraft; they were not very worried about dying, but more concerned about life after death.

It strikes me that Africans generally seem not so bothered by the cultural fears of death that afflict materialistic Europeans. Beliefs in sorcery are widespread in rural Malawi and a new witchcraft cure for AIDS attracted huge crowds in 1996. The local newspaper reported:

Thousands of people from all corners of Malawi and from all walks of life have been swarming to a herbalist's little known Chikanama village, to drink a drug believed to cure AIDS. This was produced by the vision of old Mr. Chisupe. He dreamed of this purifying herbal potion, 'mchape', made from the bark of a local tree, which would cure AIDS.

Such huge crowds came to drink his 'mchape' that the village became a sanitation risk and the government had to bring in water bowsers. Eventually the government pathologist announced that Mr. Chisupe's clients who had drunk the 'mchape' potion continued to be HIV-positive and many then died, and stressed that people should continue to observe the advice of the anti-AIDS campaign. However Mr. Chisupe was not deterred, and argued that AIDS patients also die in hospitals despite modern medicines.

AIDS challenges all social attitudes and HIV-problems have turned religious morality about abortion upside down. A gynaecologist at a Mission hospital summed up the dilemma, telling me about one of her patients:

"One girl of nineteen is surprisingly seven weeks' pregnant and has also suddenly developed galloping TB and Kaposi's Sarcoma. As the pregnancy suppresses her immune system, so the cancer, the HIV viruses, and the TB germs are multiplying without much opposition in her body, and she will die within a few weeks. If she has a termination of pregnancy, her own immunity may improve, which would slow the progress of her diseases, and she might live longer. But Christian hospitals do not allow abortions, nor do Malawian laws." She emphasized the categoric need for abortion to be offered to HIV-positive pregnant women. It should be a universal human right.

By 1999, all Malawian hospitals are reporting rising death rates of HIV-positive women in childbirth, and increasing numbers of stillborn babies. In addition, about half of the babies born to HIV-infected Malawian mothers also develop AIDS, with about 30% acquiring this virus in the uterus before birth and perhaps 20% ingesting it from the infected mother's breast milk.

The death of a baby of a wailing HIV-positive mother in Michael's clinic prompted him to write:

> "When first she moved and quickened
> I was waiting for my time.
> Then she thinned and sickened,
> Cried out her little while,
> (Never even a smile)
> Now I'm waiting for – my time."

AIDS also presents grave problems in all branches of surgery. If HIV-positive mothers are at high risk of dying from haemorrhage or sepsis in childbirth, then HIV-positive patients are also a risk in all operations.

Michael reports: "In 1999, perhaps 80% of surgical in-patients in Malawi are HIV-positive, but fewer have AIDS related complexes, Kaposi's Sarcoma, and infected ulcers and abscesses. Sometimes patients who had straightforward operations for routine conditions would not recover well or the wounds became infected, because of suppression of immunity. In any case a surgical condition has to be dealt with surgically – an abscess opened, a hernia repaired. HIV-testing is only done if the result will influence the treatment.

A young army officer presented with a potentially operable bladder cancer. The operation would be a major one and involve diverting the urine into the bowel. Knowing the high rate of sero-prevalence in the army, a test was done. He was HIV-positive, so the operation was not suggested."

During our time in Blantyre AIDS problems impinged on everybody there. When our servant was summoned to a little village of grass thatched huts at Mulanje to take his dying polygamous uncle to the witch-doctor across in Mozambique, a telephone message came that he was also needed at the village funeral of his niece, a hundred miles to the north.

Then Patrick arrived to stay in our servant's quarters: he was aged thirty two, illiterate, ragged, very thin, and his mouth ulcers were so bad that he had not been able to swallow food for a month. I drove him to the very long queue of Queen Elizabeth hospital outpatients. Unlike many, Patrick was seen by a doctor, and he was grateful for an examination and drugs prescription. However as the hospital pharmacy had run out of drugs for severe pain, his agony was prolonged for a week. Then our servant came to me and said; "Patrick is going to die. And he wants to go home to our village, seventy miles away, up in the Chikale mountains bordering Mozambique." Michael and I could not leave Blantyre. I drove them to the bus, with pain pills, and money for a taxi to transport them along the last ten miles on the rocky, mud road.

Poor Patrick sat crouched up on the bus too weak to raise his head, whilst our servant decided to keep the taxi money to pay for the funeral, because he looked close to death. This meant they would have to walk along the last miles up the steep mud road to their village. As they started their ascent into the bush, Patrick suddenly said "I cannot go on, I must lie down", and so he died. Within minutes the local people had organized a litter to carry his body the long ten miles to his village.

African hospitals are desperately short of supplies to mitigate this suffering. At one old colonial hospital, the pharmacy had only penicillin in stock, whilst all the pain relieving drugs and antimalarials had run out. In the wards, the covers had fallen off the mattresses long ago, the sheets had gone, and the whole hospital had only three blankets. Michael examined some terribly suffering AIDS patients. A dying man with a very high temperature, was crying out and shivering as his blanket was pulled back. The staff felt hopeless as there was no pethidine for the many patients who perished in such pain.

When I saw one child in the ward, I thought he was recovering from burns, but that was not so, the exposed big sores on his ankles and legs, with skin sloughing off in lumps to reveal painful flesh, were caused by AIDS. This three year old would die in agony with his flesh dropping off his limbs. Another small boy had herpes all down the side of his face and into his mouth, making it painful to drink. He already looked frightened, realising his illness was progressing. HIV has now become a leading cause of death in children as well as adults in Malawi.

Most victims die at home as WHO advises 'home based care' hopefully supported by drugs and dressings from the local hospital. Close to high mountains, where the streams swollen by the summer rains cascade down the precipices to the racing river torrents, a Malawian government hospital matron complained to me that the local home care scheme was not working at all, and highlighted the following problems:

"Patients discharged from the fee paying mission hospital arrrive here two days later wanting to lie in our crowded wards. Already we cannot cope with our enormous number of patients, so we have to refuse. The HIV-victims stay around in town, and come back here at dusk when the night staff cannot turn them away. At home in the village they have no bed, no drugs or dressings, and no food. That is why they want to come here. Our wards are now so crowded with AIDS patients that we cannot provide adequate care for the sick who could recover with treatment.

International World Health Organization policy decrees that we are not allowed to put HIV-patients in separate wards. But the people formulating guidelines on the other side of the world do not have to cope with our problems. Here only one nurse cares for a ward with ninety seriously ill patients, several unconscious and on saline drips. AIDS patients need separate shelters, so they can die in peace and comfort. This need should be officially recognized."

It seems that publicity about suffering and dying from AIDS might influence behaviour and customs. I shudder at the latest plans from World Bank for 'behavioural change units' to encourage 'health seeking behaviour' or safer debauchery. The real problems of African society are not going to be solved by running around with another western strategy, suitable for American drug addicts. What is needed is more humility and humanitarian concern from the rich world in the face of this terrible epidemic which could yet engulf Europe.

Final Journey

The AIDS situation in the rich world is very different in 1999 compared with a decade previously. New drug regimes, although with side effects, greatly prolong survival. But it is unlikely that these expensive treatments will be available in the poor world in the foreseeable future. Also the virus may change, as has happened to other infectious diseases in the past.

One day in 1994, a Polytechnic student commented to me "looking at the sprawling city around me, I think survival depends on the genes determining behaviour. About a third of the young men I meet are probably going to catch HIV with their reckless behaviour, another third of us will certainly avoid AIDS because we have no inclination to be promiscuous, and the rest could land by chance on either side of the line."

So a biblical remnant may survive with a new inspiration to change their society. It may be that the old African polygamous culture will have to give way to a new social ideal of one wife and two children to ensure human survival in Africa after all. And all this could happen in Europe and America too.

Chapter 10.   Dreams and Demons

A tourist flying into Lilongwe International Airport sees a patchwork of maize gardens around crowded villages of little thatched mud houses, fringed by a few swaying banana trees. Here, the people of the Chewa tribe struggle to grow diminishing crops in an overworked soil and a few trees survive in small dark clumps around graveyards.

These old trees have a special spiritual significance because they form a link with the souls of ancestors. Traditional carvings often depict the tree of life in which the extended family in this world is a part of a greater family tree beyond the grave. By ancient custom, little prayer houses used to be built deep in the forest, because there mankind could commune with the divine spirits.

The conflict between the donor 'development' dreams of rich countries and the culture of poor Africans is now sharply focussed around here. For centuries these plains of the central region of Malawi have been covered with indigenous brachystegia forests sustaining the Chewa people in harmony with nature. Thousands of wild animals used to thrive in the woodlands, and hunting was a major activity to procure food. Now, in the February rains, this land was covered with a monoculture of green maize plants, over which swooped black, long-tailed, widow birds, and cardinal red bishop birds.

My students fondly talked of their village traditions which are at the heart of African life, moulding and disciplining each new generation into the old social structure: *Chewa people settled on gentle sloping land at Tembwe, by the Bua River, and they cannot leave this lovely spot. They build little circular pole houses without windows, with a door made of grass, skilfully woven. Little children enjoy sleeping at grandma's house because she tells them stories before they sleep on a grass mat on the floor. At sunset, male elders eat their meal, under the chief's tree and discuss the village problems, whilst the women also eat in a group together outside the house. Then there are special occasions on moonlit nights when girls dance the old 'Chimtali' for the initiation rituals to ensure their fecundity in childbearing.*

However today this traditional high birthrate threatens the very birthright of these Chewa people – their native soil. In more terse sentences students mentioned some sad aspects of their culture – this idyllic rural picture of the village is framed by the sinister Nyau societies guarding ancient tribal customs.

Nyau is a secret band of dancers with animal masks hiding their real identity, and with membership limited to initiated males. Both puberty and death are important events in Chewa life, adolescence marking the change from a barren childhood to fertility, whilst death transforms a bodily man into an ancestral spirit. To be accepted as social adults, boys join the 'Gule Wankulu' dancing of the Nyau societies at initiation and at funeral ceremonies, wearing masks for rituals at graves. The Nyaus usually teach children to be very fierce, to fight enemies and wild animals, and often do not allow them to go school. The ideas perhaps reflect the fears of the forest tribes threatened by wild animals.

All my University students objected to the promiscuity of these adolescent initiation rituals, hoping these cermonies could be banned by national laws. One young man wrote: *I pity children, because I had to go to the initiation ceremonies against my father's wishes. The chief chooses a day, and dances are organized in the moonlight with abusive songs. Amid the dancing, boys are taken away to the tsimba hut in the bush, and in a brutal ceremony they are circumcised. Rituals for girls are also very harsh.* Another student touchingly defined this trauma for young people: *The initiation ritual fades away the subconscious purity of the young person's mind.*

They also explained that: *The Nyaus worship the dead ancestors as gods who will assist society in times of war, drought, famine, and disease. In witchcraft, the dead have power over the living, tragic deaths are associated with witchcraft, and anyone caught practising that used to be executed by burning.* Because of Nyau opposition to modern schools, and also because of some promiscuous initiation practices, Christians used to forbid their converts to dance with them, and today the Churches are still in a dilemma about the Nyaus, managing only a mutual toleration.

University students also considered much of their Nyau culture was a barrier to economic progress – *Villagers sometimes believe anyone who makes a lot of money is involved in some bad witchcraft practice. They think a person becomes rich as a result of harming somebody by sorcery. So many people have feared prospering in business because they may be cast out of tribal society as witches. Few shop owners know about credit and banking. This has caused many rural credit schemes to fail.*

In witchcraft beliefs, people are dominated by fear. Perhaps the real objection to sorcery is that it demotes humans to a level of social functionalism, so a person cannot easily live with intrinsic dignity, emotions, instincts and rationality. What is missing is the idea of human love, of respect for instinctive motivation, and of personal choice in private relationships.

When I left the Polytechnic in 1994, my students said in a farewell tribute: "We are all grateful, because you have opened our minds to make our own judgements. When we go around Malawi now, we look at our problems as free people, no longer coerced by our traditional attitudes."

However there are some parallels to the coercive African withcraft culture in recent European cultural fashions. Modern norms often demand that women suppress their wifely and mothering instincts and prove their value in work achievements. This is also a form of social functionalism, with academic status and work reckoned as more important than loving marital and parental relationships. Similar problems are reported with computer addicts – "Australians besotted with their jobs rather than their partners have been advised to turn off their faxes and turn on romantic love."

In African villages, sorcery cultures maintain the high birthrates, leading to so much malnutrition. By the 1990s we witnessed this increasing poverty at Dowa, an old Chewa town nestling in the hills, as we were welcomed by a British doctor and his wife. They were living in a British colonial brick house built eighty years ago, with verandahs netted against insects. The area had been rocked by earthquakes the previous year, so their home had gaping cracks in the walls as well as a swarm of bees in the roof.

Dowa town had been short of many things since the Asians were ordered by President Banda to close their shops in the seventies and then move out. This old brick hospital had been built by the British colonial government in 1931. Termites now lived in mounds beside the wards. It was a constant fight to get any essential repairs done – the autoclave for the operating theatre was missing a part, so it was difficult to sterilize instruments. Much equipment was broken.

Nsima (maize porridge) for patients was being cooked on a blazing wood fire outside the hospital. In the rains, patients had to be wheeled out of doors across the mud from the wards to theatre – and then back again post-operatively. Yet it was a cheerful, and very busy, hospital, with crowded wards and many male floor patients.

In the paediatric department, children lay dying, weakened by malnutrition. The 1989 Nutrition Survey in this area indicated that 70% of children suffered from chronic malnutrition. This was the main problem of the surrounding villages, as described by one of the Malawian University students:

People in Dowa district are not afraid to speak to me openly because I am one of them – improved health care has reduced the infant death rate, but the birth rate has not been limited at all. This is because fertile parents are esteemed but barren couples are social outcasts, suspected of sorcery. With increasing numbers of people, there is not enough food to last for the whole year.

In the four hungry months before the harvest in April, men from starving families go away to distant villages. They ask the Chief for permission to buy food, and then hoe family gardens for several weeks to pay for it. This is known as the 'Msumwa'. For one man to earn enough to feed perhaps his own family of eleven children is not a joke. He exhausts all his energy and his health suffers.

Driving south from Dowa to the blossoming garden city of Lilongwe, we entered a very different world of foreign development visions and unreal dreams. This capital city of Malawi was planned by Kamuzu Banda when he was imprisoned in Southern Rhodesia in 1958, and, until his downfall in 1994, Malawians could not openly discuss their own national policies.

This town of imposing government secretariats and embassies seemed like an alien shoot grafted on to an African family tree. Plush diplomats, sitting in guarded ivory towers, with tastefully furnished air conditioned rooms, surrounded by secretaries, cups of coffee, and fax machines, dispensed international taxpayers' foreign aid money.

These privileged bureaucrats always greeted us courteously, but they were also in a moral maze because some of them were beginning to realise that the worthy aims and lofty tones of international policies were being defeated by overpopulation here. The old foreign aid which used to support public services like hospitals, roads, water and electricity supplies, and local staff training programmes, was certainly more modest and successful. The arrogant notion that foreign government policies could change rural society and eradicate poverty, has in fact abandoned many public services to grave deterioration.

In 1990 a charming French WHO doctor's frustrated comment to me when I visited him in the Ministry of Health was typical – "twelve years of maternal and child health work has achieved nothing in the rural areas of Malawi. It is a failure. There has been no reduction at all in the high child mortality rates here, despite the very good (over 90%) immunization coverage."

Serious rural poverty affects the lives of affluent people in the cities too. In the spacious blossoming avenues of Lilongwe suburbs, we would reach the fortified homes of the rich. High fences covered with razor wire, alarm bells, and saluting guards, indicated the growing number of youths around town who could only find employment as thieves. Pick up security trucks raced by on the prowl for robbers, looking like a film set about the gestapo, with helmeted private guards sitting back to back, holding muzzled alsatian dogs. They were demons guarding the dreams.

Demons guarding the Dreams

On our visit before Christmas 1990, with the members of my Polytechnic orchestra who had been given violins, violas, and cellos by German aid, we were all invited to the German ambassador's residence for a delightful Advent tea. Entering his home was to find a world very different from the 'Msumwa' in the famished Chewa villages around Lilongwe. An old festival of Christian Europe now signalled love, hope, and luxury. It was a very real contrast to the sad fertility rites of the Nyau societies.

I was greeted with a traditional heel clicking bow and a teutonic kiss of the hand. This Ambassador was charmingly formal. We went out to an emerald green lawn where Santa Claus with a donkey was giving out presents to children. The Polytechnic students enjoyed coming here, but they were nervous of being seen talking to any diplomats. So Michael chatted to our hosts, while the boys played chess and looked at the flowering gardens with me. The ambassador made a nice speech about our orchestra on the lawn, and then we went indoors to decorated tea tables.

German advent candles were set on wreaths, and we ate sandwiches, canapes, and Christmas fruit cake, washed down with strong tea. Afterwards we sang carols, and our Chewa cellist, who was a fervent Christian musician, touchingly rendered 'Silent Night' in the high falsetto male voice which traditionally recounts stories during dancing in the village, rather similar to the recitative of European music – perhaps this kind of artistic transformation of old tribal customs may one day help to defeat the saddest aspects of witchcraft.

We continued in this spirit at our evening Lilongwe concert, with ringing trumpets and dynamic strings playing Purcell's Trumpet Tune, a quiet Nyau Funeral Dance I had arranged for strings, and Handel's 'Musick for the Royal Fireworks'. It was an easy diplomacy, for at this highbrow level the basic problems of the Nyau societies were not obvious.

Next day, at the British High Commission, beside a wispy, gentle, portrait of our Queen, tea was dispensed from a Georgian silver tea service, and the china bore our British Royal coat-of-arms. But the looming sorrows around us in Malawi could not be muted with this blotting paper of elegance.

During the acompanying British health conference, Michael, along with other doctors, was questioning the value of primary health care in the current Malawian situation. It was exhausting, lobbying donors to keep the most basic hospital services running, instead of pushing health recipes on to the poor world which were self-defeating and would soon create far worse rural problems. And by 1999, Lilongwe hospital often lacks sutures, cotton wool, sheets, elastoplast, and is so short staffed that some patients are said to die whilst waiting in for attention.

I found it was a relief after hearing about the global policies thought up in New York, London, and Geneva, to escape to the honest doctors at the Nkhoma Mission in the bare mountains arising to the south of Lilongwe. They were Afrikaaners from the old Dutch Reformed Church of Capetown, and some had worked among the Chewa people for thirty years. We enjoyed their hospitality, sharing their soup and bread. They understood that health cannot be quickly achieved in rural Africa, and that it may take several generations to change attitudes. Their hospital had pioneered family planning in Malawi.

This old Mission had indicators of the indigenous forests growing around Nkhoma a hundred years ago. Much furniture was a century old, with armchairs, bedsteads, doors, rafters, and tables, beautifully made by the early carpenters; the ceiling in our bedroom was made of reeds. Now these old trees were disappearing, cut down for firewood by the ever increasing numbers of villagers. Local streams were drying up.

We heard the mission hospital staff were worried that AIDS was being spread locally by the promiscuous tribal initiation rituals. One surgeon had become a leading ophthalmologist and noted that tumours of the conjunctiva were often presenting in such HIV-positive patients. By 1990, the missionaries were living to the daily sound of funerals with so many people dying of AIDS.

Recently a man had died at dawn, and two hours later his funeral passed by. As he had perished from HIV, the family would not keep his body for even a few hours after death – because they thought it was bewitched. AIDS also increased fears of sorcery.

Then one cloudless, crisp, March day with the dew sparkling, we made the steep climb up Nkhoma Mountain via the old mission guest house. A century ago, the Chewa people used to retreat to this plateau when the fierce, marauding Ngoni tribe attacked them, and used their hoards of stones to hurl down on to their assailants. People then faced death in battle, but are they now powerless to face the overcrowding that may lead to famine and perhaps tribal conflict again?

Not only have development policies fueled ecological stresses in Malawi, but refugees encamped here for eight years 1986-94, also destroyed thousands of trees. For fifty miles southwards from Nkhoma, the main tar road over the Kirk mountains has formed the frontier between Malawi and Mozambique, and here were half a million refugees from the Mozambiquan civil war living in UNHCR camps on the Malawian side of this road. They could not be housed in guarded camps in their own country on the other side of the road, although this could have lessened the deforestation and erosion of Malawian soil.

A person can only become a refugee outside his own nation, and this policy created problems. In Africa, these refugees were a privileged class of people, with 'rights' to free daily food, gifts of clothing, blankets, building materials, and health care, all of which combined to exceed the lifestyle of many of the poor suffering Malawian villagers around them.

One British hospital doctor was annoyed by the telephone calls he was receiving from the UNHCR staff – they complained that the child death rate in the local refugee camp was four per thousand children each month and demanded that it should be reduced to two per month. He replied angrily that the Malawian infant death rate in the district was higher than that. It was politically correct to be worried about refugees but not about local people.

The danger of banditry around the refugee camps was widespread. At one hospital Michael examined a patient with a gunshot wound in the thigh. He said guerillas were systematically burning down the villages across the frontier in Mozambique. It was a scorched earth policy to drive the people out of their country. Bandits were also coming over the frontier. When a chief's hut on Dedza mountain was surrounded by a threatening mob, an old lady came out and said he had run away ten minutes previously, pointing down the hill. The robbers ran down there so allowing the chief to come out and escape. They also were desperate to seize the food given to refugees.

Driving along this frontier road between Malawi and Mozambique, we saw many little boys holding out items for sale such as tins of donated European Union surplus butter, Norwegian lamps, and cooked mice on kebab sticks. I bought some of this butter to make a cake at home, but I still retain European prejudices deriving from the Black Death of 1348 in England, when fleas spread bubonic plague from rodents to humans – 'three blind mice, see how they run' – I cannot eat roast mice! I think nobody in Europe eats rodents, but they are a popular snack in south Malawi.

Mozambiquan problems went much deeper than the politics defined by international journalists. A Dedza student described to me his extended family living across the frontier:

Mrs. King, you do not understand, those people are all very traditional. You see they have not been educated like us in Malawi, they are not Christians, they are African pagans. Frelimo turned out all the missionaries twenty years ago. They live only with their old tribal culture. They believe that when rain has not fallen early, the ancestors are angry and old people who are witches must be killed.

When we visited a British doctor at Ntcheu district hospital, we learned that he had recently done a post-mortem on an old man stoned to death by poor villagers for this reason. The police could not easily interfere in sorcery like this, nor ban it. This was yet another example of the overwhelming problem of rural witchcraft and coercive community traditions.

I also realised starkly the dangerous struggle for survival in these crowded refugee communities when coming back along this road alone one stormy January evening in 1987, after taking our daughter, Fiona, to Lilongwe airport to return to Cambridge. She begged me to stay in Lilongwe for the night for safety, but I wanted to return to our new baby grand-daughter by the lakeshore.

So, recklessly motivated by grandmotherly instincts, I hoped to drive the fifty mile stretch along the frontier road before darkness shrouded the high Mozambique mountains, controlled by warlords, to the west. The sharp rays of the setting sun lit up the terrain of that forbidden land, long ravaged by guerilla warfare, suffusing jagged white mountain peaks in brilliant pink light. Only plants manifested the former prosperity – hedges of fir and rows of cypress trees delineated a drive to a ruined old Portuguese homestead; as masses of flowering bougainvillea and frangipanni indicated another former home with a view.

The shot-up decrepit walls of one roofless old farm, surrounded by rusting harrows and ploughs, had all been abandoned now for years, but other clusters of banana trees or huge shady mango trees, revealed that people used to live there and loved the land.

Now, by nightfall, every peasant had to leave his own tiny vegetable garden over the road in Mozambique with his wood bundle, or hoe, and the minutes of daylight were fast fading. Hundreds of refugees were dancing by the road as I drove past, but many other young men were sitting high up on the hillsides in the twilight , gazing westwards and intently looking out for bandits. In the fading light, I dared not put on my headlights, in case my car too attracted guerillas or thieves.

At last, after this perilous fifty miles, I reached the international frontier post at Ntcheu as darkness mantled the land, and my car was examined by kindly Malawian policemen, advising it was not safe to go any further along this main road. So I turned left to a seventy mile mud track over the mountains towards the lakeshore. Reaching the top of a hill, I could at last stop for a few minutes to rest and drink airport tea from our thermos. It was a brilliantly moonlit night with distant flashes of lightning across in the Mozambique mountains to the east, and

After they had returned to Mozambique; Roofless Refugee Huts

comforting to be passing the cooking fires of homely Malawian villages again, just a few miles away from bandits and guerilla attacks.

Here the interruptions were quite different as countless night-jars, sitting on the road eating insects, rose up in flight towards my headlights, around every corner, and over the brow of each hill. At last I came over the watershed on this tortuous, slippery, mud road and began the descent to the lakeshore. The moonlight reflected in the calm waters of Lake Malawi illuminated the whole bowl of the Rift Valley with an ethereal light.

When I reached our abode, how thankful I was, after this anxious journey, to return to the security of my husband and family and see our darling baby grand-daughter, Nicola, sleeping peacefully in her Moses basket. Outside the hippos were snorting and splashing in the Lake.

Gratefully too I realised that as Europeans we escaped from witchcraft many generations ago. The humanist Renaissance philosophy, the individualistic Christian values of the Reformation, and the humanitarian integrity of science and technology have replaced mediaeval fears and demons in our cultural inheritance, and effect our contemporary protection and social safety net. Instead of fearing demons, we are able to place a high priority on matrimonial and family love. This secures our lives. We should keep counting our blessings.

Chapter 11. Polygamy in Africa

'As fair thou art my bonny lass,
So deep in love am I;
And I will love thee still my Dear,
Till all the seas go dry.' – Robert Burns

It is interesting to compare European and African culture. In our tradition, emotions are channelled into private relationships. European love songs, poetry, drama, and art, have for centuries reinforced monogamy – we hope 'to fall in love, get married, and live happily ever afterwards.' The romantic ideas about chivalry and courtly love of the mediaeval troubadours put ladies on a pedestal of respect. This tradition, with Christianity, has produced Western individualism.

By contrast, in Africa, a person is first a member of a tribe. Emotions are diverted into bonding relationships within this group. Customs such as initiation ceremonies and tribal dances at weddings and funerals, reinforce a person's links with the communal group. For example a student wrote this description of the Jiya Wedding Dance in the male dominated Ngoni tribe, illustrating the village management of marriage.

The village elders are concerned about harmony in the new family, especially as regards sexual satisfaction. On the wedding eve some elderly women give a lecture. A woman is said to be loving if she can tame the man herself. Failure to manage this may result in the husband having his ego satisfied elsewhere. Outside the people sing and dance all night long, while those unable to take part in the dance sit around crackling fires and exchange jokes and stories. The men escorting the bride to her new family dance the Jiya Dance, and the women ululate: 'This is our daughter; we hope your son, her husband will keep her safely, elders of the village we salute you."

A major problem of polygamy was evident in the population pressure on the land in Malawi by the eighties. In 1986 a student told me about his own Chewa village near Lilongwe: *A husband wants his wives to work for him in the garden, and to bear many children to prove his manhood. One man has three wives and thirty-one children. They are often ragged, have little food, and do not go to school. The family land has to be subdivided between these wives and their average of ten children each.*

A comparison of families shows that the more wives per husband, the less the yield, per wife, from the maize crop. Since each wife has to grow food for her own many children, they often starve. Then a one-wife family lives in three houses, but a polygamous one needs a whole village.

One woman mentioned that thirty years ago this village was a spot in the forest. There were many deep and perennial streams, and thick forests alive with wild animals. Now, as the numbers of people have incredibly increased, people have devoured her area with villages, cattle and goats, and maize gardens. Wild animals, except for the hyena hiding in the graveyard, are almost extinct. Today this land is always bare and dry, and eroded gullies are common. There are no good crops from this deteriorating soil nowadays. Our lot is hunger and misery to bequeath to our heirs.

Western governments have mistakenly imagined that development in health or agriculture, could be achieved in such polygamous communities. The opposite has happened in the African economic decline of the past fifty years. Donor aid has probably sustained a polygamous tribal family system which might otherwise have not survived.

Malawian University students offered more insight into their own marriage traditions. They regarded polygamy as a shackle to the past. Much tribal land was tied up by this institution, to be farmed inefficiently by struggling polygamous wives. There is a big generation gap now in Central Africa with many young men and women wanting to end polygamous customs and so liberate the whole tribal land system that goes with it. Modern farming would increase food production but also increase unemployment.

However, more important objections to polygamy are the emotional ones. Polygamy is the sorrow of Africa. It gives ladies a chattel status – they are reckoned by their work and fecundity, like a horse, cow, or slave. Personally I think the polygamous wife is in a degraded sexual situation and a prostitute may have more freedom. In fact polygamy is a form of institutionalized promiscuity and should be condemned for that reason.

Older African women told me emotionally of their despair about the whole marriage system. My first encounter with polygamy was in Swaziland, a beautiful country of deep granite valleys covered in the dry winter months with brownish dried grass and little dark green stunted trees, where there might be solitary polygamous villages with five or six grass thatched huts beside the fenced cattle kraals.

On a sunny September morning I was invited to coffee by the Prime Minister's senior wife; in the gardens of her official residence, beside red hibiscus flowers flaming against the blue sky and looking across the beautiful mountains, we chatted about the problems of Swazi women. Her comments were interesting.

"You see the unhappiness of polygamy. There is no closeness in a polygamous marriage, a wife is not emotionally linked to the husband and is just used for sex and childbearing. Swazi ladies have traditionally been denied matrimonial love in their lives." This was searingly honest and heart rending – feminism and its issues seemed a strange distant phenomenon.

I replied that modern contraception would eventually end polygamy. In old African custom a mother did not sleep with her husband for two years after childbirth whilst she was breast feeding. This was the traditional method of child spacing. So he took another wife to be his sexual partner during his first wife's abstinence.

Through the maize

Modern contraceptives could both protect a mother from another pregnancy and support her continued breastfeeding, so ending the need for this old style polygamy. However modern birth control should also introduce a new idea of a marriage based on mutual love. Both birth control and new marriage customs could improve life for African ladies, and perhaps her princely spouse would be willing to listen to this point of view. We had a very engaging conversation.

A male dilemma in these unemotional marriages was revealed to me twenty years later by a gynaecologist in Malawi. She was puzzled why only 2% of the fifteen thousand ladies delivering babies each year at Queen Elizabeth hospital, Blantyre, would accept birth control. Mothers told the counsellors they did not need contraceptives because they would not be having sex with their husbands for another two years after childbirth. Then they would only copulate solely to achieve another pregnancy. On this reckoning, a man would need four wives to achieve sexual intercourse twice a year!

Younger men and women in Malawi today analyse polygamy in modern concepts. They can see it as gender inequality, as an abuse of female emotions, and of female reproductive rights. Increasingly, educated modern African young ladies opt out of marriage altogether. They agonize over the point of marrying a man who can legally marry more wives when a wife is barred from marrying more men.

Matrimonial customs are affected by the varying tribal traditions in Malawi – in the north the Ngoni, Tumbuka, Nkhonde, and Tonga, people have a patrilocal tradition – a bride goes to live in her husband's village. And as different stages of Ngoni life are denoted by dress styles, they have no initiation rituals to establish adult status at puberty.

The proud and male dominated Ngoni tribe are a clan of the powerful Zulus who left Natal during the cruel 'mfecane' of Chief Shaka in the 1820s, thousands settling as the Matabele in Zimbabwe, and other clans migrating to the northern mountains above Lake Malawi, and building little thatch houses and fenced cattle kraals.

As these Zulu/Ngoni are a cattle-herding people, a bridegroom pays a customary brideprice called 'lobola' – usually comprising four cattle, to his fiance's family. University students offered fascinating comments about their own tribal marriage problems and expressed a complexity of opinions about their own customs:

Lobola encourages husbands to be hardworking – and binds a marriage. Lobola has nothing to do with love between the marrying pair. The husband's family has chosen the wife, but does she love him? If not, they will be miserable. Another unhappy feature is that the husband has total control of the sex performances and his wish is to produce as many children as possible to show a return for his lobola money or cattle.

The traditional Ngoni man insists his wife must be pregnant regularly, in order to keep her under his control. I feel the lobola system is often like buying a person as a slave. (Ngoni young woman)

A man marries an ugly woman because she is cheap. Because he does not love his wife, he goes after other women.

Other Ngoni students commented *Rich men marry more than one wife. Without children there is no valid marriage. All the children belong to the father and the mother has no say over them.*

Polygamous sex is solely for the procreation of children. Polygamous sex is just a carnal activity. These wives turn away to prostitution because one husband cannot satisfy more than one wife in an emotional and sexual sense.

These students also mentioned the difficulties between polygamous wives: *When one wife sees she has failed to win the favour of her husband, an evil mind comes into her, so she will decide to bewitch either her fellow wives or the husband. Sometimes the wife tries to put love potions in the husband's food, and the ingredients will be poisonous and kill the man. This creates widows, and the children suffer.*

Polygamous wives usually hate each other, and some even find ways of trying to kill their fellow wives.

By contrast in the southern regions of Malawi, the Yao, Chewa, and Lomwe tribes of Central Africa are female dominated and matrilocal, with ancient customs enforced by the male Nyau witchcraft societies. Groups of fierce Nyau dancers wearing masks, goat skins, and feathers, can often be met along the main road near Lilongwe. Their masks represent the powerful ancestral spirits moving from the forest to the village to demand appeasement from mankind. They will perform Gule Wankulu dances at the Initiation ceremonies for adolescents, but such practices were continually condemned by my university students, agreeing that the barbaric rituals affected the whole cultural and social attitude to marriage. It was perhaps difficult for a couple to establish a relationship based on mutual respect and loving care after the initiation experience in childhood.

Students commented: *All Chewas must perform the Nyau society rituals. Any man who does not have his children initiated in the ancient ceremonies, sometimes with brutal circumcision and rape, will be beaten by the Nyaus. These Chewa ceremonies are child spoiling devices leading to early pregnancies and quick marriages that do not last long.* A widely held opinion.

Many Yaos are Muslim, and those girls often feel insulted by the status of polygamous wives in their own culture. It condones male promiscuity. One woman student noted *A Yao husband can make more valid marriages during his first marriage, but a wife cannot. He is supposed to live at his wife's village but he may easily go elsewhere.* A husband though has an authority in a Muslim marriage.

However, this nuptial situation does not prevail uniformly in the woman led traditions in south Malawi. At the foot of the high Mulanje massif, are little villages of mud and thatch houses, with some chickens and ducks, and a patch of maize. Here among the Chewa people, there is a fascinating aspect of female self-rule. When a man marries he goes to live at his wife's parents' home, which is known as a 'Chikamwini' marriage. This situation is said to be like the waters pounding the lakeshore, with the polygamous wives anchored on various bits of sand, and visited by husbands coming and going from their lives like the waves crashing on the beach.

One student told me about the families at his own Samela village at Mulanje in 1986: *About a hundred and eighty people live there in small family units around the mother, with the eldest son as leader of the family. Each family lives in a cluster of houses, with a group of sisters as a ruling sororate at the core of the village. In this tradition of inheritance, the family land is subdivided between the daughters. So the high birthrate has caused a land shortage, and about two thirds of Samela family gardens are now of less than one hectare.*

The marriage bonds tend to be rather loose. These 'chikamwini' husbands are outsiders to marriage, just visiting sometimes. So most households are headed by a polygamous wife, usually with seven or more children, and it is the wife's brother, the uncle, of these children, who makes decisions about them. Although there are equal numbers of young boys and girls at Samela, many young men choose to leave this village, so less than a third of the adults there now are male.

These 'Chikamwini' marriages were intriguingly and varyingly described by my students: *At the wedding, the husband comes to live at at his wife's village, which makes the wife the head of the family and the man lives in fear that she will dominate him; as he has no land of his own, he works in her parents' garden. The Chewas encourage marriage at a young age. The kinship system is matrilocal, and each group is headed by a female.*

Other students commented; *A Chikamwini husband is often regarded as a servant when he goes to live at his wife's village. He has to pay for his sexual rights by working in his wife's garden.*

And; *The polygamous Chikamwini wife is an inactive sexual partner, often exhausted with all her work to maintain her homestead. So frustrated husbands go around with other ladies, and adultery and polygamy are common.*

Yet another boy noted; *The Chikamwini husband is treated harshly. He is expected to do all the farming, build houses for his father-in-law, and he has no total freedom. The husband is not in charge of the children. As a result of having no say in family matters, he neglects the children, and does not appear to love them. They are taught by their uncle how to plough, how to behave, and if they go to school to read – no more.*

There were similar sad complaints from Lomwe students; *The wife must prepare food for the husband before she can eat herself. True love is missing, especially for the man. Statistics show that malnutrition is much more common in the children of polygamous women.*

A paediatrician in Malawi confirmed this opinion in her overcrowded under-fives clinic which often served a thousand children a day: "When I examine yet another of the hundreds of starving children, the mother's face is a good clinical indicator. If the father loves her, she will want and love his baby, and so will struggle hard to ensure that infant's survival. But often children are malnourished just because mother does not care about baby – since the father did not marry her for love. So she is not so interested in the child and the prognosis is poor."

The real objections of ladies to polygamy are human and extend right across Africa. In 1985 we drove to Tanzania. On the bare plains of the north west, the Masai people were herding their cattle, walking majestically as if on stilts across the vast plains. With their brightly coloured robes, they have the superior attitude of nomads. The plains belong to them and they wander at will.

We camped beside the road to Arusha. As darkness enveloped us down on the ground, the clouds in the sky thinned for a moment and the summit of Mount Kilimanjaro was suddenly visible, with its snow capped peak glistening high above us in the brilliant rays of the setting sun – like the dramatic lifting of a bridal veil.

I heard less attractive revelations about the local marriage traditions next day. At the meeting of the East African surgeons, three Tanzanian nursing matrons sat at our separate ladies' dinner table. They were tearful as we discussed African polygamy. In hospitals they saw the misery and violence of polygamous homes on a daily basis, and they begged us expatriates to try to do something about this dreadful custom in Africa. It seemed that the polygamist often wanted to humiliate women. They mentioned a Tanzanian professor who had brought back an English wife from Britain, and then degraded her sexually and racially by having an African wife in the home too.

Furthermore polygamy should be criticized as institutionalized promiscuity which is dangerous in the HIV-epidemic, because a link between polygamy and AIDS has now been observed in most Malawian rural hospitals. By 1996, the majority of the female patients in one medical ward were dying of AIDS. The ward nurse commented to me that "These patients infected with the HIV virus are all polygamous wives, and polygamy is spreading AIDS." She went on to explain how this happens: "No man can be a proper husband to more than one woman; if he has more he cannot offer her the love and sympathy that she wants as a female. When a husband marries another woman, the first wife resents this, so she starts running around with other men. This is human nature, and it is true all over the world. So a polygamous wife easily catches AIDS which is then passed to the other spouses in the household."

It became clear to me that international human rights definitions ought to respect the emotions and instincts of every man and woman. People clearly do not find dignity, self respect, sexual ecstasy, or joyous relationships in polygamy. How can a marriage possibly exist between several people when there are no other securities to bolster it such as economic, psychological, and spiritual factors?

The hetero-sexual HIV-pandemic is spreading most rapidly in countries with a polygamous tradition. Yet donor governments ignore polygamy when considering AIDS policies. Academic development studies which classify 'female headed households' by their food, water, education, or work, have also easily ignored polygamy.

Even a young Ngoni man defined his own society's problems: *Old African culture does not respect a person's instinctive human nature.*

However, polygamy is disappearing slowly. Modern young people see Christian marriage based on a loving relationship as a happier way of life, especially with contraception.

In fact birth control and economic factors will eventually effect the demise of polygamy, and this is the social change that could bring rapid economic progress and private happiness in African societies. Nevertheless the donor community has not shown interest in polygamy as one of the most important cultural problems of Africa.

The international implementation of monogamous marriage laws would go a little way towards the world-wide demographic stability so essential for human survival in the next century.

Daily tasks

Chapter 12.   Land of Fire

"Smooth runs the water where the brook is deep" – Shakespeare

The word Malawi in Chichewa means 'land of fire' and grass fires have swept across the East African woodlands in the dry season for thousands of years. Visitors are often enthralled by the lines of fire zigzagging up the mountain slopes on moonless winter nights. But these grass fires replenish the fertility of the land by only consuming frail trees. Robust, fire proof, hardwood, indigenous trees survive in the African savannah, and many huge ones are centuries old.

Only a few trees in some areas survive from these old forests today, mostly on inaccessible and very steep mountain slopes. Five miles east of Blantyre city, Chiradzulu Mountain rises three thousand feet very steeply as a giant granite citadel, starkly silhouetted against the brilliant sunrise. It is often shrouded by the heavy clouds and violent thunderstorms which come in from the Indian Ocean.

Many times we made the three hour climb, up varying steep paths, to reach the long ridge of rocks at the summit; on the way we walked up past the few ancient patches of forest still surviving in the ravines of the high mountain. Here is the home of African eagles, calling stridently as they soar over the peaks; but they too seem endangered. We would often see bare patches where trees had recently been felled. The enormous girth of the remaining stumps would indicate that these recently cut trees were many centuries old, their massive roots spreading like tentacles in the hillside, holding the soil and retaining the rain water in spongy damp soil.

Climbing mountains in south Malawi, we were frequently not alone. Continual 'tap tap' sounds indicated poor people hidden in the woods around us, illegally felling trees with axes. Over our time there, the tree cover thinned, and in a few years most mountains near Blantyre lost their green mantle. At last, starkly bare, like Ndirande mountain, they radiated more heat from their glinting granite rocks.

Yet the people living around here were still culturally influenced by the ancient hunting way of life in Central Africa which was closely dependent on the indigenous brachystegia forests, the home of thousands of wild animals. I once heard an old man describe his great-grandmother's story about her own mother's experience as a little girl.

She had walked in the 'Great Trek' of the huge and fierce Ngoni tribe, a clan of the Zulus of South Africa: in 1828 they fled northwards from the cruelty of their Chief Shaka in Natal, going through Zimbabwe where many settled to be called the Matabele, then across the Zambesi River to reach north Malawi as the Ngoni tribe. This was the story bequeathed in the family folklore:

Our Ngoni warriors who led us two thousand miles through the unending forests, used to shoot buck for our meals, and many wore animal skins. By night, I lay close to my mother as we slept around a high blazing wood fire. Looking out into the dark forest beyond the circle of our warrior sentries, I would see the moving dark silhouettes of huge animals passing by – elephants, buffalos, and rhinoceros; and then some brilliant pairs of moving, gleaming, jewels – they were the eyes of lions on the prowl.

On these mountain walks, it often struck me that the hypocrisy of the foreign aid policies for Africa is obvious in two separate and quite incompatible ideas which are dear to the heart of European and American television viewers – foreign notions of 'saving trees and wild animals' and 'saving babies' in the tropics take pride of place.

Mountain storm

Although my university students expressed continual worry about increasing population pressure on their woodlands, they were fearful in Banda's time, if they spoke openly of any deterioration in Malawi. African government policies were formulated by development experts in Washington, London and Geneva, among others, designed to be acceptable to rich government politicians, and also appeal to wealthy voters with electric luxuries. The rich world tried to call the tune in Africa and it had to be a crusading hymn about 'development'.

As early as 1982, one of my university students secretly described the deteriorating tree cover in his own Mpama village, near the foothills of the massive dark citadel of Chiradzulu mountain: *Before 1970, the Sangano hills of Chiradzulu were densely covered with trees, and traditional houses were built with tree poles. Materials for building and thatching used to be abundantly within reach of my village. There were many high indigenous trees here, often centuries old. The Mlombwa tree grows along the banks of streams, whilst the red hardwood Mbawa and Napiri trees grow on the upper slopes of Chiradzulu mountain.*

At my village the people are Yao, and polygamy is common. Often one man may have eighteen children with three wives. The population density by 1982 is three hundred and ninety seven persons per square kilometre and today no family planning is allowed in Chiradzulu district. Scarcity of firewood is now so great that people often use maize stalks as fuel. But these do not burn for long before the fire dies out between the three traditional 'mafua' stones around the cooking fire.

Huge quantities of wood are used for the ritual four day beer brewing process of the Yaos. Many trees also have to be felled to provide fuel to fire the brick kilns, and the development projects of foreign donors require much local brick making. The old traditional pole houses of the village are now being replaced by houses of brick, requiring many kilns to fire them as well. Charcoal making is a source of income for many poor people and several carpenters are short of wood to make window frames, furniture, axe and hoe handles.

The 1970s saw a huge deforestation around Mpama. Denuded hills today bear mute testimony to the overcutting caused by high human population density. I was told by government forestry officials that soil losses are a hundred times greater from deforested land than from timbered areas, and water losses are sixty greater from denuded soil. So streams are now drying up for much of the year and rivers are falling. Where the soil has eroded, maize yields are deteriorating.

Witch doctors also worry that indigenous trees and plants used for African medicine have disappeared permanently from river banks. They now have to go to the streams high up the slopes of Chiradzulu mountain to find them.

In our African custom, the trees in graveyards are sacred, and collecting firewood there is forbidden. Cemetery trees can only be used to make coffins. The local council has tried re-planting areas of Mpama with fast growing blue gums. Nguludi hill is one of the places recommended for afforestation. But 80% of the crowded local villagers asked for this hill to be left alone because they want to plant maize up there.

Steadily the ecological ravages in south Malawi worsened. Development projects to build better houses, schools, health centres, and businesses, all consumed trees to fire more bricks. As we stood on Chiradzulu mountain in 1992, we counted no less than fifty-eight wood fired brick kilns smoking in the Chiradzulu/Zomba plain below. In the end, the poor rains of 1992 finally led to an ecological crisis in the whole district around the Chiradzulu and Zomba massifs. Everybody depended on the pure rivers flowing down these steep granite mountain slopes. As more trees were steadily felled, so the streams diminished. Heavy rains now flowed straight off the hillsides, without tree roots to hold the water in the soil like a sponge and keeping the brooks flowing through the dry season; but now with so few trees around to shade the earth, water also evaporated quickly in the blazing hot sunshine.

My article in the local newspaper mentioned this plight: "Zomba town faces another water crisis now. The piped water system from the Mlunguzi river, flowing off Zomba Mountain, was constructed forty years ago to supply a town of 4,000 people. Today the urban population of Zomba has increased to 60,000 citizens all needing to drink a minumum of three litres per day. So 90,000 litres of drinking water alone is required daily. And this does not cover all the other water needs – water to bath in, water for washing clothes, dish washing, sanitation, and watering vegetables.

Two years ago the Mlunguzi dam up on Zomba mountain went dry so bowsers brought water from the Domasi and Thondwe rivers flowing from Zomba and Chriradzulu Mountains. Now both these two rivers and many other brooks are drying. Several tales are told of this 1992 water shortage. Some university students bath at midnight because there is a trickle of water in the tap then. Out in Zomba and Chiradzulu areas, village bore-holes are dry, so women have to walk miles to find water and carry it home. One new rural clinic has already closed because its bore hole has failed.

Of course farmers are complaining about dessication. With streams now only trickling, upstream villages have been trying to save their water by building small dams. This has angered thirsty downstream villagers who are rumoured to have destroyed upstream dams forcibly at night.

Rivers no longer flow as far as Lake Chilwa and the huge marshes which supported hundreds of fishing villages there are parched. The level of Lake Chilwa is dropping daily, and the whole Lake may dry up this year, although this has been reported sometimes in the past. Are immediate water saving measures the real answer to this problem? If parents continue to beget large numbers of children, then they too will be born to thirst."

Events proved however that this dessication was not just a one year event in Malawi, it was to become regular. Two years later, in 1994, the next water shortage in Zomba was so serious that residents of the crowded townships were being told to go home to their villages. Reaching home though, they found the local streams and water boreholes had all dried up too, so they became ecological regugees. And this problem was not confined to south Malawi. News arrived from the central region that so many trees had been felled in the mountain forest reserves at Mua, that streams were drying up there as well.

There are ecological limits to human numbers. Do couples today have the right to procreate as many children as they want in this overcrowded situation? Perhaps individual rights should be reformed to ensure survival of the whole community. By 1997, one leading Malawian politician, had already thrown down the gauntlet about these problems in a crowded Blantyre township electioneering speech, saying: "As long as our birth rate grossly exceeds our death rate, then poverty alleviation in Malawi is a non-starter".

By 1994 widespread rural water shortages impinged on the city of Blantyre, with its water supply piped from the Shire River. As the level of Lake Malawi was falling, the Shire waters also dwindled. The level of this Lake has fallen the past, so clear cause and effect cannot be defined.

However thousands of people were coming into Blantyre, leaving villages where there was little water. They crowded the pavements all day, many living there, and making a living by selling a few items. Others built mud and thatch shelters around the townships.

Cycling home from a Polytechnic lecture as darkness was coming, one cold July winter night, I became frightened. On open land beside the road, there were dozens of newly arrived, tragic families, many with little children, sleeping out in the open on the freezing night. They were making fires of leaves and twigs to keep warm, and to cook their sparse supper. But where had they suddenly sprung from? I wondered where they would sleep? How would they find food?

The wide extent of these problems became evident when bad news was announced at our Blantyre Wildlife Society's monthly meeting. Apparently other crowds of thirsty villagers had migrated to the banks of the falling Shire River waters. After millions had been spent by foreign government donors on fencing Liwonde game park to preserve the animals, the Malawi government had now announced that anyone could go and fish in the river this year – and would probably cross to the other side to the Park as well, to find firewood and food. Now it seemed that the German project to restock Lake Malombe with fish would suffer as would the trees and wild animals in the game parks.

When this news was grimly announced, the attitude of the seated rows of Blantyre expatriates was weirdly unrealistic. "Why can't the forestry department enforce the laws to protect all the trees on the towering Ndirande mountain in Blantyre?" they asked. "Why have the forests on so many other nearby mountains disappeared in the last five years?" The newly arrived foreigners on the spot did not see that the rapidly multiplying population of Blantyre inevitably caused mass deforestation. But in the cold light of day are there really any laws enforceable against starving, cold, thirsty, people?

This Wildlife society was busy assisting the government with a project to replant denuded areas with seedlings of some of the old hardwood trees of Central Africa. The Malawi government has had a good record in its re-afforestation policies for thirty years, giving out tree seedlings free of charge in the villages to plant at the beginning of the rainy season. But colossal efforts at tree replanting in Malawi over three decades have failed in the face of this population avalanche. Conservationists have come to ressemble King Canute telling the sea tide to retreat.

Projects teaching school children about tree planting have to be equally blamed because the birthrate problem has hardly been recognized in school teaching. The World Wildlife Fund lobbied the Malawi Government to sign to the principle of 'protecting forests' as late as 1996, but it would be impossible to enforce this.

If the human suffering was heart breaking, the ecological destruction was as sad. For years we enjoyed family walks with our daughters up through the forest reserve of Michiru mountain in Blantyre, to dip in the pool of a cascading river near the summit, and enjoy a picnic up there. One day in 1991 it was a shock to find our lovely pool had disappeared.

The joyous, rushing, brook of water from mountain springs had dried up and gone, and all that remained was a pool of stagnant water in a rocky cleft. This was now the only watering place left for the birds and animals. So the fleeting thump of a running herd of little buck, the footprints of the stealthy leopards and hyenas, and the troupe of huge baboons defiantly barking from a tree branch against our progress along a path, would all vanish now.

Michael wrote these words of comfort, dedicated to those wanting to "save trees" in 1993:

> When next you see
> The stump of a cut down tree
> Do'nt say someone misbehaved
> Think of the baby that tree has saved.

> The father views his cold and hungry child
> Then – the tree growing wild
> Needs must he will up and fell it
> And build, or burn, or sell it.

> So, Rejoice when you hear the axe
> See the branches on their backs
> For housing, cooking, needs like these
> The good Earth provides the trees.

Chapter 13.   University Teaching

"Only lies need the support of Governments, truth can stand alone" –
Thomas Jefferson's defence of press freedom.

Frangipanni branch with the intensely irritating Chitedze (buffalo bean) creeper on it.

Flanked by our hospital and the police station in Blantyre, close to the traffic roaring on the main Kamuzu highway, was the Polytechnic, housing the three University of Malawi faculties of commerce, engineering, and technical studies. Its square buildings donated by the United States were softened by the curved lines of the library, dining hall, and engineering laboratories, all added by British Government aid.

Gardens of flaming bougainvillea, red hibiscus, yellow oleander, blue acanta, and scented frangipanni, beautified the campus. The backdrop was Soche mountain, with its summit still crowned with a little dark rainforest. In the rains, herons would perch on our dining hall roof, like storks foreboding new ideas, new life in Africa.

Every year the numbers of Polytechnic students increased and my classes in the faculty of commerce became more crowded. By 1988 I was teaching a hundred and fifty undergraduates in a delapidated hall without enough chairs. The vast majority were young men – our course with its good job prospects being the first choice for school leavers.

These students came up to the University from all districts of Malawi, – more than half were Yaos, Lomwes, or Chewas in the matriarchal tradition of South Malawi, whilst the overwhelming Ngoni, Tumbuka, and Tonga 'Boys from the North' felt greatly superior in their male dominated tribal culture.

In 1980 I was appointed university lecturer in human behaviour at the Polytechnic where I worked until we retired from Blantyre in 1994. My local contract with the University of Malawi was renewed every two years, to give lectures in human and industrial psychology to the first year students, and to supervise the research projects of the third year undergraduates.

As a British woman, wife, and mother, I felt unable to sound authoritarian or even expert in teaching these excellent pupils, the brightest school leavers in Malawi, who would certainly be the future leaders of their people. So I had to take a different approach saying "I am a foreigner and this is your country; I can show you how to study topics, but only you know the real problems of your nation, which it is your privilege and duty to define." Because I respected their situation, and more importantly our differences, they opened their hearts to me.

I was already aware of the growing rural problems of Malawi, and in their research projects, I had to help students to define these problems honestly in the face of grave political intimidation. I used to explain to British external examiners that research had often been done in fear, and a student would be in personal danger if his or her work was ever published or he/she was identified.

It was some achievement for any Malawian to be critical, because everybody had to believe absolutely the slogans of President Banda that 'my people have food, clothes, and a roof that does not leak'. We also had to affirm the equally questionable universal aid policies thumped out by United Nations organizations and international donor governments.

I soon realized that my Malawian colleagues on the academic staff were worried about President Banda's government. They disliked the increasing poverty and starvation, the rumours of misappropriation of state funds, the high birthrate and the ban on birth control, and the tribal land system. The political tortures and murders of the seventies and eighties shocked all of them.

Since I am naturally outspoken about unjust regimes, I could not be seen openly associating with my colleagues, otherwise they would be targeted as dissidents. So I ventured to criticize President Banda's govenment quite openly in lectures, and this freed Malawian individuals who were my academic colleagues, from looking publicly subversive.

However, for thirty years (1964 – 1994), President Banda received strong moral support in America and Scotland because he had trained as a doctor in Meharry USA and at Edinburgh, universities which acclaimed him as 'one of us'. Foreign support probably kept the Banda regime in power for twenty years longer than it would otherwise have survived. However he was a cold war ally of the West, and communists had become established in neighbouring Mozambique since the seventies, taking an active part in the thirty-year civil hostilities there. Wounded Mozambiquan soldiers were often brought across the frontier to Michael for surgery, and sometimes they were wearing Russian uniforms.

Over my fourteen years there, I saw Polytechnic students gradually muster an intelligent opposition to President Banda'a absolute rule. Quite simply, African dictators could afford to bulldoze public opinion. To stay in power they needed to suppress their male rivals.

Clever Malawian politicians saw the distrust of the polygamous 'Chikamwini' wives for their menfolk in south and central Malawi. And so if a robust man queried President Banda, there was a swift reaction from him – 'My cohorts of thousands of dancing, beloved, tribal Mbumba (women) will know what to do with him'. And this summary female justice allegedly despatched errant men of any tribe – especially from the male dominated Ngoni and Tumbuka northern tribes – to be punished, imprisoned, tortured with electric shocks or 'thrown to the crocodiles in the Shire River'. This was the fate that might await Malawian male critics. Hell hath no fury like that of embittered polygamous women.

I felt that intelligent definition of rural and commercial problems was the catalyst for change in Malawi. The student projects revealed the unfolding tragedy, due to the rapidly increasing human population. And in 1988 I recorded these typical topics – one boy studied inflation in his village: rising prices meant that many people could no longer afford to buy soap or salt.

Unemployment was causing many qualified young men to seek jobs in South Africa. By 1996 only 2% of boys leaving Nkhata Bay secondary school in north Malawi could get any job or course of training. One student even feared to go to his home in the Thyolo area near Blantyre because he might be attacked by the Nyau witchcraft societies which opposed education and progress.

Polytechnic students had wide and responsible interests. Several organized church choirs in the Blantyre townships, so I started to give violin, viola, cello, and double bass lessons at break time. Such gifted musicians easily learned our Western notation and string playing techniques. The German and Chinese (ROC) embassies gave us some fine instruments, and we soon embarked on Purcell and Handel trumpet suites.

We needed no conductor. Our leading violinists would invigorate the rhythm by their bowing, with a verve picked up by the rest of the orchestra. It was like the natural drum beat of singing and dancing in the village. Students said music was a part of sorcery and magic in old African custom. So the inculturation of ancient music and dance into Christian liturgy, and the development of music as an art form, is desirable.

String Orchestra

Walking through the butterflies fluttering around the shrubs in the Polytechnic gardens, I was often uplifted by the beauty of the flowerbeds of flaming African marigolds and blue salvia against the backdrop of the Blantyre mountains. The stark, jagged, deforested, granite skyline of Ndirande Mountain towered over the the Blantyre shanty townships around its base, where thousands lived – up to seventeen people in one little mud and grass thatched home, so my students said. It was easy for Europeans to be bewitched by the wonderful natural beauty of Malawi and to be unaware of the growing multitudes of the desperate poor.

However, President Banda's supporters gradually realized the weight of criticism, even of opposition, felt by educated young Malawians at the

Polytechnic. Although several sons of Banda's government ministers and powerful political cronies were in my classes, the tide for political reform amonst the Polytechnic students swept along steadily, year by year.

By November 1988, the government's intimidation of the Polytechnic opposition began when all traffic stopped on Kamuzu highway for a Remembrance Day rehearsal. I had to park our little car in the neighbouring QE hospital and run across this main road to give my lecture, just dodging the presidential motor cavalcade which was roaring by at speed. I gave my lecture quietly as usual, little imagining the political framing that would soon be thrust on us all.

By lunchtime our departmental secretary phoned me nervously – "Dr. King, did you see any students on the highway this morning?" – No I had not, in fact there were no adoring crowds around the Malawi congress party chairman as his cavalcade raced by. It was that which was the problem!

Soon the police summoned our principal to ask why an alleged small group of students had been seen making rude gestures at this chairman as he passed by, and they demanded that these culprits must be named and expelled. No student was identified during a week of continual police inquisition interrupting our lectures at the Polytechnic, although it was rumoured around the campus that some top government politicians had been sighted ouside our girls' hostel a month ago!

Eventually this notice was displayed: *Serious concern is hereby being expressed that when HE the Life President's convoy passes along the highway, students and staff do not line up along the road, and the few who happen to be around do not even clap hands. Our traditional way of paying respect to our beloved Leader is to stand and clap. May I advise that when the convoy is passing, no attempt should be made to cross the road.*

Few undergraduates wanted to applaud a regime which tortured and murdered their relatives. Four boys were expelled for printing a satirical poem 'Come, Come, And Mend' poking fun at the President's 'CCAM' or the Chitukuku Cha Amai Malawi womens' league. This CCAM was the club of educated ladies organized by the President's companion, the official hostess.

However British diplomats were willing to listen to university undergraduate opinions. I often transported Polytechnic student leaders hidden under blankets in the back of our van to meet Foreign Office officials or BBC reporters at our home in Blantyre. These officials travelled to us in cars flying the Union Jack. A Blantyre police inspector who had thirteen children lived next door to us, and was always watching us.

In 1989 my students were inserting secret comments in essays for me as follows: *Dr. Kamuzu Banda is telling Malawians that there is enough food, while many are dying in poverty. It is unfair.*

Our people are becoming dependent on free food handouts. In our country famine cannot be eradicated by free food.

We have been denied our right to know what tax-payers' money is spent on – we know it is used for immoral purposes, like buying instruments of torture, or fancy cars for Ministers.
Organizations like WHO and UNICEF do not give our country a chance to solve its own problems.

We could make a very good world if we put all our effort into controlling the population increase here with birth control. The giving of free food has made people lazy, so they no longer have to work to provide for their children. They can marry early and have as many children as they want.

Other students commented: *The issue of free condoms has destroyed our community; people are living freely, doing evil, and AIDS is spreading rapidly. Is it moral to bring food aid to Malawi to ensure first child survival, when what follows is famine ?*

Secondary groups in Malawi have been politically useful. Young men in the Young Pioneers are indoctrinated with kamuzuism, requiring them to idolise President Banda and his political party. Personal friendships are rare – boys and girls live in suspense of each other.

Polytechnic staff were some times criticised for lack of research. Academic promotion normally depends on published papers with the quip 'publish or perish'. But in President Banda's Blantyre it would be 'publish **and** perish' – and so become another meal for the crocodiles. In such a dreadful situation, we quietly tried to face the real, unutterable, problems that western governments also did not want to envisage, for a perilous decade.

I have little respect for foreign inspired research about development issues based on rich-world assumptions and blinkered to the real problems of African society. This is pseudo-research, but academic development libraries worldwide are full of such reports and aid policies are based on them.

With my open criticism of the Banda rule, I was surprised in 1990 to be promoted to be course tutor at the Polytechnic. Undergraduates said the Banda regime did not deport me because of the respect the people felt for my surgeon husband, so I must go on speaking critically.

I wrote in my diary: "April 1989: Students are handing in their research projects secretly behind the hedge. Everyone is afraid of Big Brother now. The special branch of the police is watching us."

"November 1990: Poly students are studying starvation in Mchinji, witchcraft, women in Chiradzulu, and the fact that only President Banda's eight hundred tenant farmers in central Malawi are allowed to grow burley tobacco which is easily dried and has such a good sale. A boy describes his village near Lilongwe where there is no industry and no economic progress at all. It is now dominated by the Nyau witchcraft societies conducting bad ceremonies at graves, eating human flesh. The Nyaus try to prevent people sending their children to school. They allow parents only to register their children at school; after that they must stay away."

Tobacco Bales

By 1989, President Banda was behaving like the mediaeval English King John levying the compulsory tax of scutage. Students reported from Ntcheu in central Malawi that *the Chief blew a whistle to call all the people. He announced that every family must contribute one kwacha to buy a leopard skin for the President's Christmas present. The people are angry because they cannot afford this and they know the money will go into the private bank accounts of top people.*

That year compulsory contributions to the President were being extracted from everyone. At Chikwawa a levy of 'free contributions' was made for the President's crop inspection tour. A notice in the hospital required clinical officers to pay K8 (about £3) each out of their meagre salary, and similar money from all government employees. The President announced that each time he visited the Lower Shire Valley 'things get better and better' although even the state controlled newspaper admitted that a third of the inhabitants now had almost no food. Even so these people had to donate K16,000 to the President, arbitrarily taken from civil servants' pay packets.

By December, at Thyolo hospital there was a notice announcing the amount that everyone must 'donate' to the Womens' CCAM club. This money had not yet been deducted from wage packets but the threats were there – a few women had been imprisoned for refusing to join CCAM. Michael's payslip for May 1990 had a 'special recovery' of K12.50 (£5) which was to be paid to the President without his consent.

The heart-breaking accounts I received of students' relatives being tortured and murdered in prison became frequent. These were typical of dozens. At the end of term exam in 1990, one girl waited until last to finish writing before coming up to me very fearfully to hand in her script. She was afraid to be seen speaking to me. In whispering tones she said she was a relative of a man who had been politically murdered. Her uncle, a senior civil servant in the Foreign Ministry, had recently been tortured to death, apparently in Lilongwe police headquarters. Her aunt was still imprisoned. "Why does the British government support President Banda?" she asked, pitifully.

Then I heard from another student all the worries about his relative, the first qualified Malawian pilot, who had also been terribly tortured in Lilongwe police headquarters. His relatives were told that he was imprisoned 'entirely at the discretion of His Excellency the Life President, and could only be released when HE signs a document allowing this.'

One evening in April 1992, after all our many protests to British diplomats and to Amnesty International, the telephone rang one evening as Michael and I were watching a video of 'The Forsyte Saga'. It was the British doctor at Zomba speaking quietly and nervously – "I hear that pilot suddenly died today. The prison authorities are not going to inform his family. Elspeth, please would you go and tell his wife. She has not been allowed to see him for six months now. We do not know why he died."

The saga of sorrow never ended. We never knew why he was arrested or how he died. By 1991, I started receiving warnings that I too could be in danger if I continued to denigrate these abuses publicly. Our daughter Fiona came out to stay for Christmas and begged me to be more careful as she had heard from local charities of my public remarks about President Leg-Irons Banda. Catholic priests also kindly warned me about strange car accidents that seemed to happen to protestors. However, retreat would be more dangerous than advance now.

In January 1991, Michael and I were invited to have lunch with Lord Tonypandy, formerly Mr. George Thomas, Speaker of the House of

Commons who was visiting Malawi. Half an hour before, my students publicly gave me a message "donor governments must please insist on multi-party democracy in Africa".

It was a very hot day when we arrived at a garden restaurant in Blantyre. I wore my green batik cotton dress, and the British High Commissioner arrived with his honoured guest. They had come straight from Sanjika Palace, and commented that the President was becoming senile with periods of loss of talk and a puffy face. Personally I think he was choosing not to hear their humanitarian protests.

They enquired kindly about Michael's surgical work and asked what help was needed. In Lord Tonypandy I found a kindred spirit – he was a Methodist preacher and interested in Christian morality and the young people. He asked if I felt safe talking openly and wondered why I could say so much against the regime. He commented that private personal morality is the basis on which national human rights are built. He had read Amnesty International reports about Malawi and was horrifed.

I told him I had brought these reports back from Britain hidden in my orchestral music, and circulated them in the university. He had also read an African economic report quoting Malawi as being the poorest country in the world in terms of rural income. We had much in common, and although he was keen to come and speak to my class about morality, it could not be fitted into his programme.

But terrible intimidation continued. The brother of one of my students was pounced on and this was reported by undergraduates in a secretly circulating newsletter:

Saidi was a businessman in Mangochi. In November 1991, some women were arrested on their way from a Jando ceremony on account of wearing the trousers traditionally worn by Yao ladies at initiation. Saidi bailed these women out of jail. He complained to the police that the women should never have been arrested in the first place. If Asian women are allowed to wear trousers as part of their tradition, why shouldn't Yao ladies be able to wear them to Jando? The police were so enraged at Saidi's eloquent defence of basic freedoms that they locked him in prison without any charge. After a few days, he was beaten so savagely that he died. Is he not a new martyr to freedom?

A month later I went to the little bookshop in Mangochi. I was introduced to Saidi's young widow. She was a beautiful girl of 28 wearing a black veil over her head, and now trying to support her baby by running this little shop. It was just around the corner from the prison where her husband had been brutally put to death, almost within earshot. She was just another new political widow, and she had to continue to live near her husband's murderers.

This secret student newsletter in February 1992 continued: *It would be possible to extend this list of martyrs almost infinitely, especially if we include the innocent people held in apalling conditions without trial in our many detention centres; people who, even today are being brutally beaten, held in chains without food, sometimes dying of hunger. Almost every Malawian has family members or friends who have been thus treated.*

For many years undergraduates had actively politicked in secret. They objected to the foreign backing for President Banda and his government, and to the American political support for the womens' leagues in Malawi. But as late as 1991, academics, churchmen, and doctors, in Edinburgh still proudly feted Kamuzu Banda as 'one of us' – were they ignorant about the thousands suffering and dying in his prisons in Malawi for many years now?

At last in 1992, open opposition increased. Following the Catholic bishops' courageous Lenten Letter openly criticizing the government in March, Polytechnic boys marched down the Kamuzu highway singing inflammatory songs about the regime, and demanding democracy. The consequences were savage. Police raided their hostels with tear gas, and arrested dozens. Nearly a hundred were badly beaten and then released, and twelve were detained for a month.

Six of my first year boys were taken to a remote police station for interrogation where screams muffled the questions of "who were the ring leaders?" And "what political movement was this?" Odd quotations in my lectures from the Magna Carta, Thomas Jefferson, and Abraham Lincoln, were now a cause for them being tortured, with the force of five men being used against one. It began with slaps and blows, and then became much worse; one student's eardrum burst when his head was punched. Then tortures were effected with instruments until they became unconscious. Lastly they were all asked to sign a confession that they were 'involved in politics'.

They were brought to Blantyre's Chichiri prison for a further month, but it was so full that they were housed separately in a punishment room. Here they were not assaulted but they saw one terrible case. An escaped prisoner who had been recaptured, was brought into their room at three in the morning, made to sit on the floor, and three guards forced his left arm into a manacle with his right ankle, and his right wrist with his left ankle. As the leg iron was only big enough for the bottom of the leg, the full force of three policeman was needed to squash the wrist in with it, which prohibited the flow of blood to the feet or hands. Within a minute the man was screaming with pain, and he was kept like this for six hours. Prison staff told them that some bad prisoners had to be kept in that position until they died.

The boys saw more than fifty pairs of leg irons in Chichiri prison, many of them newly bought. They also saw dead bodies being carried out daily. This only confirmed other terrible reports from prisons in Malawi.

When Michael visited this prison he found two hundred and seventeen convicts, and eight hundred and eighty nine more prisoners on remand being held there indefinitely; they had never been brought to trial in court. Nearly a thousand prisoners lived in a room called the shamba, originally built for two hundred convicts. At night they had to sit up back to back. The police could not see that a widespread reaction to thirty years of torture and oppression was already happening. It was the undergraduates who had the courage to say openly what everybody was feeling and soon the citizens of Blantyre rioted.

Belatedly, the Western donor governments insisted on democratic change. Soon, at the insistence of the new British High Commissioner, the International Committee of the Red Cross arrived to inspect gaols and stayed for two years. Two of their Swiss delegates came to call on us at home, and one of them was, like Michael, a member of St. John's College, Cambridge. It was a great relief for us to be able to talk openly to them at last about the political cruelty in Malawi, and to hear of unconvicted men being set free.

Later some released prisoners came to us at our home and asked me to go with about thirty others, all together, in a convoy of five cars, to meet these Swiss members of the Red Cross; because they were afraid to be seen going on their own. How humbling it was to realise that not just the very brave Polytechnic boys and girls, but thousands of Malawians, had tried to challenge the brutality of Dr. Banda's government. A few like these men, had luckily survived their terrible ordeals.

One of these prisoners had been arrested in 1965 at Karonga, sentenced to eight years imprisonment, but was afterwards not released but incarcerated without trial for another twenty years, many of them in dungeons and in leg irons. I felt unworthy when he courteously opened the door for me, and insisted I must go first. I could only wonder, why had people in Britain given so much prestige to governments like this?

Teaching in an African University was a privilege. Students identified for me some of the real problems of their societies, such as the initiation ceremonies, and took action. Today there is a real generation gap in Malawi, and in Africa generally. Ageing leaders cannot achieve development with their adherence to a an ancient cultural tradition of polygamy. witchcraft, and high birthrates, but the students, together with all educated and professional Malawians with ideas of social change, certainly can. Their leadership is needed to steer their people to a new future.

In Europe we admire soldiers and pilots who defend their own country against foreign powers. In Africa similar, if not much greater courage is needed by African undergraduates to defy their own traditions and their own leaders, in order to realise a new and greater vision for their own people. They were an inspiration in darkness, and the hope of the future in Malawi. They are the beacons of the day.

Chapter 14. The Blantyre Riots

By 1992, the people's opposition to President Banda's thirty years of dictatorship boiled over. The political intimidation and murders, and the suppression of justifiable complaints about food shortages or bullying officials reached a crisis. People in Blantyre rioted. At noon on Wednesday May 5th, 1992, many roads were blocked off by strikers and grave trouble was obviously coming. I hastened to buy enough food to last us a day or two, and Michael quickly collected the newly printed copies of our book "Story of Medicine and Disease in Malawi" from the Montfort Press after lunch, before returning to the hospital for his afternoon clinic.

By mid-afternoon the sounds of gunshots and the smell of teargas floated over a mile towards our home from Ginnery Corner, which was the site of both the Polytechnic and of Queen Elizabeth Hospital. The police came into the Polytechnic gardens and were intimidating students and shooting at the upstairs windows.

By late afternoon Michael was also trapped in the hospital by rioters and police were letting off tear gas in the grounds. A baby even died of this. I was terribly worried when he phoned and urged me "Stay at home, I will come back when I can". The hospital staff were marooned in the wards.

Soon the commotion spread to the streets around our home too. Noisy crowds gathered on the road below our garden, to defend the nearby Bishop's house from the government militias. It was the recent Catholic

The Old Town Hall, Victoria Avenue, Blantyre.

Bishops' Lenten Letter protesting at government abuses that had made the public bold enough to demonstrate. They blocked off our road, throwing stones at passing cars.

At last, Michael arrived home for tea, having left all our books in the ward in case our car should be burnt. He had driven in a convoy of doctor's cars out of the hospital, and then managed to pass through the rioting mob in the road below us. Together we ate supper to the increasing sounds of gunshots and shouting crowds only fifty yards away from our kitchen door. I was so thankful that Michael had come back safely that I hardly heard the shots. But my sense of security with him around was not to last very long.

Soon he had to return to the QE to help with the casualties starting to come in. I was afraid for him now. Would he be attacked by the angry mobs stopping and stoning cars along the road below us? We painted some red crosses on large sheets of white paper and hastily stuck them on our car windows. I made sandwiches and a thermos of coffee for him to take to his colleagues. I was terrified for him going through the furious crowds and the lines of police gunfire again. So he drove off.

In the road just below our house, he was stopped by the mobs, who were threatening to stone our car. He told them who he was, and how he was on his way to operate on people who had been shot. One rather amazed and drunk man pulled his free outpatients ticket from his pocket and shouted "Mr. King is my doctor, he cured me", and another called out "He is like the Roman bishops, on the side of the poor against the rich." And so he was allowed to pass through safely.

I stood in our garden just above this road, hearing the noise and shooting as he went along in the darkness. I was stricken with fear. But soon the telephone rang - Michael said he had reached the hospital safely! He described the scene above and said he would not be coming back for a very long time because dozens of frightful gunshot casualties were now pouring in, brought there by relatives or brave ambulance drivers.

I was entirely alone in this terrible hour, afraid for myself, afraid for Michael, afraid for the absolutely stricken peoples around us. A struggle was under way between the citizens of Blantyre and the government. What could I do? I turned off all the lights in our home for safety and went to sit outside in our garden.

The stars of the southern cross seemed to twinkle as I heard the clamour on every side. Then I decided to phone Sheenagh in England, to tell her of us. She was comforting, saying - "You went through all this twenty five years ago during the riots in Kuala Lumpur, Mummy, when we were little children with you; you will manage now."

As night fell, President Banda's special henchmen, the Malawi Young Pioneers, came out as agents provocateurs, shooting up the rioting crowds all over the city. The crackles of semi-automatic rifle gunshots went on without a break - eight o'clock, nine o'clock, ten o'clock - so many poor people must now be injured Feeling completely alone, I wondered what to do for the night. Should I go to bed, or should I stay up, so that I could run away if rioters or, more terrifyingly, the notorious Malawi Young Pioneers came in here? Where could I run to? There was no sanctuary. I decided to lie on my bed fully clothed and slept fitfully, with the gunfire continuing unabated across the city and townships to the midnight hours before subsiding.

At last, at three in the morning, came taps on the bedroom window. Michael was back! After operating on fourteen patients with gunshot wounds, he had to snatch three hours of sleep before going on duty again. He said our road was quiet at last, but with an awful lot of debris lying along it - stones, rocks, broken glass, tree trunks. At last I felt safe again, frying an egg for him quickly before he could rest. But soon the sun's rays began to pierce the eastern horizon, silhouetting the towering Ndirande mountain peaks, and heralding Blantyre's blackest time.

This next day started quietly and we decided to drive together to the hospital at dawn before the rioters came out, and then I walked around to the Polytechnic to give my scheduled lecture. I had to stand by my students. But already protesting crowds could be heard farther down the main highway around the clock tower.

All one hundred and fifty of my students attended this class, they said they felt safer with expatriates around, and in these civil disturbances I decided to teach an easy topic. Then the awful shouting noise in the street came nearer, drowning my voice, and I had to stop. We all went down to the road to see crowds of poor people looting a supermarket owned by President Banda. Dozens of thin, ragged, unemployed, youths were running away with food and goods from the shelves. Law and order had broken down. We could not continue with our lectures in this situation, as the students were fearful of another brutal police assault on the Polytechnic again.

So I walked around to the hospital operating theatre to see Michael, just as the dreaded Malawi Young Pioneers were arriving in the highway.

Dozens of gunshot casualties were already there for only four surgeons - two British and two Dutch. I decided to walk home now, because it would not be safe to drive our car. I chose to avoid the road altogether and go along by foot paths near a river, through maize patches and clumps of blue gum trees. Dozens of people were now fleeing beside me, many youths were running as fast as possible clutching stolen goods, and panic was beginning. A young clerk from medical stores told me he was afraid the looters would invade there, so he had locked up and gone. He said he had put his red tie in his pocket so that no one would steal it. The rioters had threatened that anyone wearing a tie was suspect, to be classified as one of the

Ndirande Mountain with the crowded township at its foot

rich. Then several Malawian young men going along in a group, came up to walk with me and said "Mrs. King, please feel safe today in our city, we will escort you along this mile long route all the way to your home now." And so they walked with me along the paths and I waded through the streams with many other fugitives.

By the time I was half way home, I could hear the grim sounds of loud gunshots close behind me, coming from the main highway outside the Queen Elizabeth hospital and the Polytechnic. The looting crowds were being attacked. Slowly I neared our house. A policeman with a rifle stood at the entrance to our drive, guarding the house of the chief of Blantyre police who lived next door. I greeted him with "Good morning, how are you today?" - hoping he would not shoot me!. He replied quite nicely "Our people have many sad problems, you can see that." However I decided not to take a cup of tea out to him.

So I came home safely, to coffee made by Peter, our cook. I sat down in the peace of our beautiful drawing room, but still I could hear the violence spreading, with barrages of gunfire in all directions right across the city. Michael phoned me to see if I had arrived safely saying there were bad riots with a lot of bullet wounds in Limbe town on the south side of the city, and there had been another riot near us outside the Mount Soche hotel, which proceeded to Namiwawa township near the President's palace with looting and assault. Government cronies were said to be a special target. Then crowds of angry people came down to the eastern side of the city from the sprawling Ndirande Township, where a quarter of a million people lived in shanty homes around the bare and deforested Ndirande Mountain.

Later Michael was told that the militias were shooting at people indiscriminately. The operating theatres were short staffed because there had been intimidation by rioters. So the medical assistants and nurses who had been able to reach the hospital had to manage more than seventy seriously wounded patients.

One sixteen year old boy had been shot as he was walking to school. He was injured in the jaw and chest and was bleeding heavily. He told Michael "Now I am going to die". Half an hour later, he did, after falling off an unattended trolley in the sluice. His injuries were too grave for his life to be saved, but there was no one to sit and comfort him in his final moments. He was the only wounded patient to die that week, seventy three more patients were admitted with gunshot and panga wounds mostly needing operations.

At last, after another eight hours in the operating theatre, Michael came home for just two hours at two o'clock. I gave him an omelette and coffee in bed. Shooting could be heard all that time, but we were now too exhausted to be afraid of that. At four o'clock Michael had to start operating on casualties again, not returning until three in the morning, completely exhausted. By dusk on this second day of rioting, I could still hear continuous gunfire. The militias were apparently shooting out in the townships around the city of Blantyre.

On the third day, at dawn, leaving Michael asleep for another hour, I decided to cycle to the Polytechnic. I arrived feeling very hot and bothered after pedalling as fast as I could, before any crowds came out. My students were fearful, watching out of the windows all through the lecture, nervous of another police raid. Only a few weeks previously six of them were terribly tortured in Chilomoni police station, after their demonstration against the government. It was difficult to concentrate on anything academic so I told them about the casualties and the lack of staff needed to save so many lives.

Throughout these riots, events were reported on the BBC World Service, but not on the Malawi Broadcasting Service. My academic colleague, a lecturer in biology had been arrested. Police had marched into our Polytechnic staff room to 'pick him up' on the first rioting Wednesday afternoon. He was now in Chichiri prison next door and we did not know what was happening to him; even his wife was not allowed to see him. Four years later he received considerable financial damages in a court of law for the bodily assaults he received there.

Two of my third year research project students had also been arrested on their way to post a letter the previous afternoon. One of them was ill with TB. They were imprisoned without trial for several weeks and I had to decide what to do about marking their work and unfinished research projects for the official University assessment. It was all sad.

Officially it was announced that only a hundred people were injured and twenty two died in these riots. The real numbers would never be known.

That Friday afternoon Michael had to catch up on normal surgical emergency patients; he did a pyloric stenosis, an incision and drainage, and a stricture that had been waiting for two days, and by dusk he could at last come home to rest and have a quiet tea. Eventually, he had a full night's sleep for the first time in three days.

On Saturday, we so enjoyed a gentle time at home. Michael worked at his sculpture, I marked student projects and gardened. We heard that many of the victims shot by the Young Pioneers were not rioters, but innocent people walking along the road to work.

On the following Tuesday I had to help one of my students leave the Polytechnic quickly after my lecture because he feared for his life. We passed a van which he said the special branch of the police had used to take him and eleven other boys to be tortured six weeks ago. Furtively we drove to the bus station, I paid his fare to Lilongwe, and waited with him until the bus set off.

Back in the university staff room, I was told that the special branch of the police from Lilongwe was now coming into the Polytechnic. My lecture notes with odd quotations from Magna Carta, Thomas Jefferson and Abraham Lincoln, had been seized and taken off to Lilongwe police headquarters! The following week we heard on BBC that the Paris club of the G7 rich countries had cut off all aid to Malawi because of its human rights abuses. Why was this not done twenty-five years previously? Why were the rich governments of Europe and America so keen to support African regimes like this?

After these riots, parliamentary democracy and the rule of law were foisted as ideals on the struggling Malawian poor by the rich world governments. A year later in May 1993, huge crowds of Malawians voted in orderly fashion for a multiparty political system. Michael received only one casualty during this mass political exercise - an old lady queueing to vote, fell over in the crowd and broke her collar bone.

However in 1994 a new State President and government condoning the old polygamous tradition were elected. They could not remedy the underlying poverty problems of Malawi, because donor governments were still paying the piper to call a political tune which does not advocate a population policy.

Democracy in itself does not solve problems if the people do not perceive them. There is an urgent need now for educated and professional Malawians to lead social reform and change.

However public understanding has been increased with the new press freedom required by the foreign donors. There are now several outspoken national and local newspapers, although radio broadcasting is still controlled by the government, and is the only source of news for the illiterate masses.

Chapter 15.   District Hospital Surgery   MK

Every month I visited several two hundred bedded District hospitals -a pleasant change. An hour or so driving from the city of Blantyre through rural areas, across streams and with mountains on the horizon, would bring me to a warm welcome in their crowded, dusty, compounds. A Specialist visit was an event and they made sure it went smoothly, many patients were seen, and a lot was done.

In 1994, after working in Blantyre for eighteen years, I was on my last British Aid contract. Blantyre, although still a garden city, was becoming more crowded as desperate young men flocked there in hope of work. Even though it was rewarding to teach in the new Medical School, at times it seemed that their training was a touch removed from the realities of what was possible in the declining economy. We wanted to live in a rural area of Malawi, and work in the District Hospitals.

With this in mind, I renovated a derelict, heavy, old caravan. This had stood immobile for two decades outside the Queen Elizabeth theatres. Donated originally as a blood collection van, termites had destroyed its wooden skeleton leaving only the thin sheet metal covering. It almost fell to pieces on the way to our home. Over the next two years, while rebuilding and fitting it out, we pondered where we should go. The northern region was the poorest, least crowded, and a beautiful area of Malawi and had no specialists for a population of two million. We were given permission to live beside the northern Lakeshore and towed the caravan the four hundred and fifty miles to this lovely place.

Over the years the wheels have slowly sunk into the red soil. We have put up a thatched shade and planted banana trees and local flowers. We stay for nearly three months twice a year. Rotary International pay my air fare and assist with expenses and donations to hospitals. We cook fish bought from dugout boats on a paraffin stove, living by the sun and with a candle at night. A monkey troupe comes by twice a day in the tree tops, and butterflies and bright sunbirds flit across the glade. We paddle in a home made canoe to buy fish, bread, and fruit, seeing the red beak of a malachite kingfisher beneath a bush, or a shy green backed heron creeping down a rock to the water's edge. Fish eagles keep sentry on high trees overlooking the lake. As we negotiate the various rocks, there are flashes of blue from the fish in the clear water.

In the district hospitals, experienced clinical officers can deal with most straightforward emergencies. They do all the Caesars, hernias, ectopic pregnancies, and fractures, as well as treating the medical cases. In the past, many district hospitals had expatriate doctors – mainly Dutch and British. Increasingly the posts are being taken over by newly qualified Malawian doctors from the Medical College. Much of their time is occupied with administration when most of them would prefer to be doing clinical work with patients.

I see patients with these clinical officers and young doctors, and we assist each other in the operations. When in the region, emergency cases are referred directly to me, rather than travel the hundreds of miles to Lilongwe where they often arrive in a bad condition. Non-emergency cases are saved for the next visit.

Letiswe, aged forty, was one such patient. She worked in a Mission making 'Likuni Phala', a fortified flour of maize and soya fed mainly to malnourished infants. She herself was wasting away, unable to keep food down, vomiting for the past year, and spending increasing time off work. It looked as though she had advanced cancer of the stomach or oesophagus. Examining her with the British mission doctor however, there was a hopeful sign. When shaken, a splashing noise came from her distended abdomen, indicating an obstructed stomach outflow, possibly non-cancerous. In the world of the rich, Barium X-rays and gastroscopy would be done to find the cause before operation. In north Malawi these are not available, so it was arranged that we would operate on the next visit to the mission. Such major operations were not usual there, the most common proceedure being Caesarian section.

The greatest immediate risk to a patient is often the anaesthetic, not the surgery. Anaesthesia is given by locally trained clinical officers, usually safely and fast. From the start we had problems with Letiswe. The tube which should have been draining her distended stomach was not working. The drug to paralyse her vocal cords had been given but it was difficult to insert the anaesthetic tube in her trachea. She wasn't breathing and was becoming blue. Her heart would stop if it didn't receive more oxygen. Eventually, by using a piece of wire inside the anaesthetic tube, and bending it, I was able to insert it. We could now inflate the lungs and she 'pinked up'.

Her stomach was indeed very large. The cause of the obstruction was a narrowing of the outlet from the stomach into the duodenum, due to scarring from a chronic duodenal ulcer. Normally the outlet would be two fingers wide, her's was about the diameter of a thin pencil. A simple widening proceedure was done and the vagus nerve was cut. Dividing this nerve to the stomach decreases the production of acid and would allow the small ulcer to heal. Six months later in the shed where she was making the flour, I did not recognize her, she had put on so much weight.

Peptic ulcers have been traditionally associated with the stress and worry of modern life in rich countries. Many assume that in the simpler rural poor world, these factors are absent and the incidence of this condition would be less. In fact it is quite common, and obviously far more basic worries are always present in poverty – the fear of food shortages due to poor rains, of sickness in children, and of envy and bewitching by neighbours.

The fear of being bewitched is ever present – 'who, not what, can be causing my illness?' The sing'anga is consulted in the majority of surgical conditions, resulting in delay. His scarification marks are usually present when the skin is being cleaned for the first incision at operation, as in this patient:

A fifty-year old farmer's intestines had become stuck in his long standing hernia (rupture in the groin). Very painful, it produced intestinal obstruction, and he was vomiting. He went to the local sing'anga with his brother, and was given leaves to eat and marks were scratched over the swelling. After four days he was getting weaker, and was taken to the nearest hospital. Here the chief clinical officer was unhappy to operate and sent him to me by a five hour journey over bad roads in a rattling Land-Rover.

On arrival, his shocked condition was improved with intravenous fluids. The gangrenous and infected loop of bowel was removed, the ends joined, and the hernia repaired. He remained very toxic but we were hopeful when on the fourth day his bowels started working and he could take sips of water. The septicaemia increased however and a week later, as I was doing a ward round, he died in his brother's arms – "It is God's will" he said fatalistically.

A common and dramatic cause of large bowel obstruction in Africa is twisting of the colon, associated with the high fibre diet, and rarely seen in rich countries. The twisted loop becomes distended with gas and fluid, and the patient comes in hugely blown up, with the abdomen 'drum tight'. In about forty percent of cases the cure can be equally dramatic. A stiff lubricated rubber tube is inserted from below. If it can be made to negotiate the twist, everyone is rewarded with a gush of gas 'et cetera', the abdomen deflates like a balloon, and there are smiles all round. Surgery should then be performed to prevent recurrence. An emergency operation is needed if the deflating proceedure fails, as in a forty seven year old veterinary assistant, who arrived saying "I think I have a twisted gut." At operation part of the bowel was gangrenous. This was removed and a colostomy made. At the next surgical visit to his district four months later, we operated and took down the colostomy and joined the ends up, restoring him to normality.

In children, intestinal worms can cause obstruction, It is bad enough seeing a four inch long round worm being vomited up by a sick child, but having to remove fifty or so writhing about at operation through an incision made in the small bowel can bring waves of nausea to the surgeon hours later. Most of the time these worms do not cause symptoms and are felt in the bowel by chance at operations for other conditions, such as in this twelve year old boy. The history was confusing, he had been to the sing'anga, he was sick and probably had malaria. But also he had signs of local peritonitis and a vague lump in his lower right abdomen. He could have an appendicular abscess or a sealed typhoid perforation of the small bowel.

At operation there were two white rubbery lumps which could only be parially removed, and it looked like Burkitt's Lymphoma. This is a common tumour of children which sometimes responds to chemotherapy. I happened to have some vials with me so a week later he was given a course and then went home. Unfortunately when I saw him six months later the tumour was much larger. It had either recurred or had not responded.

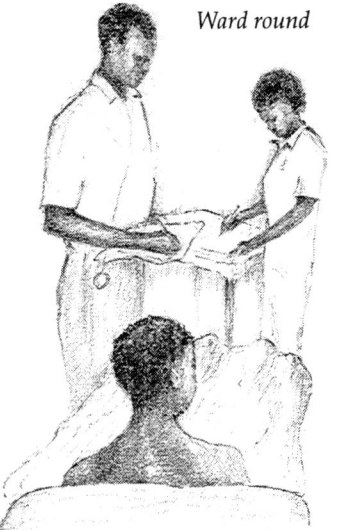

Ward round

Burkitt's tumour presents more commonly in the jaw, and a four year old miserable boy with a grossly swollen face due to Burkitt's was one of the first patients seen in the new Millenium. The supply of suitable cytotoxic drugs is restricted due to decreased health budgets, so all such patients have to be referred to one of the two Central hospitals for treatment. Free travel warrants for bus travel used to be given to such patients, but this is no longer affordable.

I had to leave the distraught father to try to raise money and persuade members of his family to accompany the patient for over a day's journey and stay in the capital city while this child's fate is decided. This was during the growing season when everybody is needed on the land if they are to eat later in the year. I doubt if he will be one of the hundred and twenty or so cases treated this year.

In rural hospitals, the doctors and clinical officers naturally have a reluctance to operate on obvious tumours, preferring to leave that to a specialist surgeon in the central hospitals. A malignant tumour is likely to bleed, be impossible to remove, or recur. Patients may die during or after the operation. Relatives will more easily accept death after medical treatment. If a patient dies from surgery or anaesthesia, the relatives and the community will query whether the operation was right. Would it have been better to await the eventual death?

Much of the cancer surgery brings temporary relief only. In district hospitals fungating breast tumours can be removed leaving the patients with a clean scar, even though the tumour had a deeper spread. A most poignant patient was a forty year old mother of five children with advanced cancer of the rectum, causing partial obstruction, pain, and bleeding. She sat on the floor, breast fed her crying baby, handed him to her husband, and climbed on to the operating table for us to do a palliative colostomy.

Another patient, a thirteen year old girl had a rare skin condition, Xeroderma Pigmentosum, – although she was black, sunlight caused multiple skin cancers to break out on exposed areas. She had a large cancer on her lower lip which required half her lip and chin to be removed, and a flap made to repair it. When she went home, it looked as though she was permanently about to whistle, but she and her mother were happy. Inevitably other tumours will occur.

Some cancer operations require blood transfusions and it is not easy to obtain HIV-negative blood. Self donation can be used on occasions; blood is taken from the patient a week before the operation, and the patient makes up the loss in that time. Without cross matching or HIV-testing, it can be retransfused. We did this in one seventy year old man for a prostate operation. By mistake HIV-screening was done and he was positive. He was the oldest HIV-infected patient I encountered.

Emergency autotransfusion is often used, as in Ulipa, a ten year old girl who fell from a stationary lorry. Over the next few hours she became paler and had increasing abdominal pain. She was obviously bleeding from a ruptured liver or spleen. She made the two hour journey safely to the mission hospital where I was working that day, although going into shock on arrival. At the mission, this sort of operation was uncommon, and so the theatre was crowded with some of the midwifery students in training. Her abdomen contained almost three pints of blood, this was scooped out and poured through a gauze dressing to get rid of clots – it was then tipped into an opened pack of saline infusion, and retransfused back. Her enlarged 'malarial' spleen had two deep ruptures in it, and was removed.

Steep coast and dugouts

Messages about emergency patients reach us in different ways. At night, the sound of a Land-Rover coming up the hill, its headlights illuminating the trees beside us, heralds the driver walking down the rutted path with a note. Once when canoeing to the south, I saw a figure jumping along the rocks and waving to us. He had a message about an emergency patient being sent from a hospital 200 miles away. As our hospital phone was out of order, the other hospital had phoned the Post Office with the clerk writing down the message – "a patient is being sent with stomach abstraction". Many hours later we were operating on a man with intestinal obstruction.

This touching letter was received from a young man with bilharzia, a parasite that causes bleeding and obstruction in the intestines and bladder:

Sir, This is at midnight of the dated. I have woke up because I cannot sleep. Life loses its meaning a lot with bilharzia larvae and eggs in my blood vessels. Why keep on living? Am I to survive and live on taking some kinds of pills every fortnight when I feel the disease is tough on me? Shall I ever get married, sure not in my present condition. The abdomen bubbling like little African women are doing their pounding business there. Am I waiting to meet my doom where I should retire and join those who are spending their days below the surface of the earth where there is no sunbathing in a morning of a cold winter? We were able to offer him the new, non-toxic drug, Praziquantel, which had just arrived, so giving a real chance of a cure.

Witch Doctor's compound

One patient came with a letter from a herbalist sing'anga stating "This patient has 'bule',(large abdominal tumour). She has been to several hospitals but they have failed to treat her. Please operate immediately." She had a huge benign fibroid of the uterus, the size of a seven months pregnancy.

We have visited several herbalists and witch doctors; some have hospital compounds with separate mud huts for men and women enclosed by a reed fence, a pharmacy hut where roots and herbs are cut up and infusions made, and a hut for healing services Some herbal concoctions undoubtedly have pharmacolgial actions but control of dosage must be difficult.

Hunger drives many people to 'overdose' during the mango season in

December and January. The fibrous pith may clog the intestines, needing removal. As a harmless side effect the pigment stains the palms and soles of the feet a striking yellow.

This next patient was also probably driven by hunger. In the hot, low lying, Shire Valley, parents brought their miserable, four year old, pot bellied, son describing his continual diarrhoea. When I attempted to examine his rear end with my finger, it was not possible because of pain. Under anaesthetic a few hours later, I could feel he had an anal stricture or narrowing. Forcibly dilating this released copious fluid faeces. His abdomen then deflated a little, but now felt extraordinary – like a bean bag. Further dilations allowed extraction of hundreds of black beans. The medical assistant cried 'Mlambe' (baobab tree). They were seeds from the baobab fruit eaten for the pulp that surrounded them. The anal stricture had prevented them from being passed normally.

Another youthful anal problem presented fifteen years late for his follow up appointment. He had been born without an anus (which is not so uncommon). Seventeen years ago an emergency colostomy had been done, and his mother was told to bring him after two years for anal reconstruction and closure of the colostomy. She had probably died and he had been brought up in the extended family situation, with no one knowing another operation was possible. The belated operation was done, and changed this young man's life.

Proper follow-up is very difficult in the poor world. If a patient is happy after an operation, he sees no reason to return. There is no routine birth or death certification.

One of the more dramatic life saving operations is draining a blood clot from the skull after head injury. This has to be done speedily; as in this next patient operated upon in a lakeside hospital.

A twenty eight year old man had fallen from his bicycle hitting his head and was semi-conscious when admitted to hospital. He was doing well until a week later when he developed weakness of his left arm and leg and started having fits. No investigations were possible or necessary, the signs were typical of localized pressure due to a clot. Instruments had to be improvised since the hand drill was blunt and a chisel was used to make a small hole in the right side of the skull. Dark old blood that had been pressing on the brain was released. The next morning he was moving his arm and a few days later he alarmingly demonstrated his recovery by doing press-ups.

Work in district hospitals is more relaxed than in the bustling central hospitals; there are goats and chickens wandering about, and relatives cooking on wood fires. Rural folk have lower expectations that their sickness can be helped by Western medicine, even if it is available. The doctor or clinical officer in charge usually remains cheerful, in spite of poor salary, in his very difficult role. He has to make sure there are enough maize and beans for the kitchens, sort out disputes among staff and give out their wages, check the hospital vehicles are not being misused, and perform autopsies on dead bodies brought in by the police. And all this has to be managed perhaps after being up part of the night delivering a baby by Caesarian section, or doing a lumbar puncture on a patient with suspected meningitis. A visiting surgeon with his specialist and narrower field of vision eventually departs with a greater respect and appreciation.

The resilience of the staff was brought home to me one night in a hospital at the end of a mud road. I had been called in to a small girl with abdominal pain. There was one nurse on duty in the paediatric ward of twenty four beds with seventy five patients, plus the mothers there; she also had to look after the male ward. There were eight babies on drips, some receiving blood transfusions for severe anaemia due to malaria, four were in her office, two on the table where there was a better light. I examined the child on a bed which also had another sleeping child and mother, there were two more mothers and children underneath, and one between the close packed beds. There was no soap to wash my hands afterwards. The nurse explained she had to use washing powder.

And she said so with a smile!

Chapter 16.   Sunrise and Sunset

Returning from leave in Britain to our home in Malawi was always a joy as my diary recorded in 1989 "an intense golden shaft of light beams into our plane – it is the brilliant dawn illuminating the vast continent of Africa. Below I can see the river Nile and the wadi of Sudan. In the course of several hours we pass over the Ethiopian and Kenyan highlands, across the volcanic mountain craters of Tanzania, and down the Great African Rift Valley to Lake Malawi, landing at Lilongwe airport. Happily I walk outside to see the distant blue mountains, the parched yellow lawns, and the warm wind blowing up from the dusty central plains. The bougainvillea and oleander flowers are all transformed by this intense sunlight – it is good to be back.

We go home to Blantyre, to a warm welcome from Peter our cook, with a very local supper of fried chambo and mangoes. Our colonial house seems enormous after the cramped homes of suburban Europe."

A message had been sent to Peter whilst we were on leave, by the poorest patients in the wards, asking for Michael to come back to look after them. It was touching. Next day I too received a rousing Malawian welcome from Polytechnic students, and in town the hungry beggars outside the vegetable market danced a greeting to me singing "Mai King – ten tambala".

However during our later years in Blantyre, the escalating problems of the people around us began to affect our home life too. The currency devalued, and there was worsening poverty and disease.

By the time the rains arrived to drench the dusty soil, the solstice was coming. Christmas was at midsummer, a time of lashing storms blown in by fierce winds. Witches believe fecund ancestral spirits descend in these rains, hovering over gardens, to promote seed germination and also vital human procreativity.

The showers soon produced a green landscape of maize patches, lush gardens, and fruiting mango trees in December. The rains heralded more than plant regeneration, because the dampness of the termite mounds of our lawn stirred procreative instincts. Just after dusk each night, millions of these winged insects would arise to find a mate. Lights were dimmed by the clouds of flying termites, and we sat at home in darkness for an hour, or our house would have been carpeted with discarded delicate wings which they shed before mating. At dusk the Blantyre street lamps were surrounded by crowds of barefoot, ragged boys catching termites and doing rather better than Oliver Twist. They were a welcome food, high in protein. Mounds of wingless termites were on sale in the market at Christmas, looking rather like black shrimps. This, along with mangoes, might be an additional relish to the nsima in many homes.

On rare occasions the termites swarmed during the day, and once we witnessed an extraordinary feeding frenzy in our garden. As the clouds of termites weakly fluttered upwards, Ant lions (dragon fly like insects that feed on the wing), hovered and darted too and fro, pouncing on them; then from the sky swifts suddenly swooped, scything through this cloud of insects. The frenzy lasted for about five minutes and the air was full of gentle, falling, dismembered, wings of termites.

On Christmas Eve our daughters usually came to play carols with us in our crowded hospital wards, where more patients were lying on the floor than in beds. The orthopaedic ward was the most cheerful, and we managed 'Joseph dearest, Joseph mine' beside an AIDS poster advising people to 'maintain your sexual partner'.

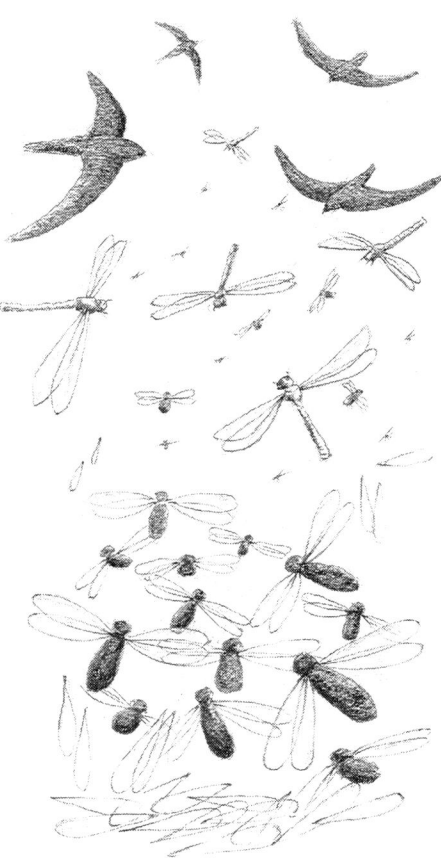

Termites, Ant lions, Swifts

In the AIDS/TB wards, the vitality of most patients was ebbing as they lay dying on the floor, gazing in hopeless apathy. Yet they too responded to the spiritual message of gentle carol tunes.

However the crowds of sick children with malnourished mothers in the paediatric ward presented a musical challenge. It was difficult to find space to set up our music stands, and the commotion and howling was unceasing. We would start playing our repetoire of carols, and then gradually an effect like Haydn's 'Farewell Symphony' would happen.

One by one, on Christmas night, these tiny suffering babies, often six to a cot, would stop crying and become interested in the sound of violins and cello playing 'Silent Night' which has a universal appeal. At last silence reigned as we played several different descant arrangements. Ragged mothers lying on the floor would call out "Eia, eia, – play it again".

Music was only a brief respite from distress. Peter, our cook, said his family in the Chikale mountains were desperate by Christmas. Most of their grain from the last harvest in April was consumed, so they had only cassava leaves to eat before sleeping, and were too weak to walk thirty miles to buy maize.

I also remember a British friend complaining that her parrot, which would eat only peanuts, had no food. In 1990 the peanut crop was poor along with the maize, so there was nothing for a hungry, choosy parrot.

The shortages of the nineties affected us too, and we could no longer be fussy. I wrote to our daughters "First we had no petrol and had to cycle everywhere, and then last week there was no bread so we had to eat cake instead, like the French kings and queens. Now our problem is toothpaste, which disappeared from the shops weeks ago. There has been no toothpaste on sale here for two months now, and we will have to make our quarter of a tube last for nine more weeks until we come home on leave. Strangely nobody in Blantyre seems to have nasty breath or nasty teeth!

Vervet Monkeys

In our garden, with the tree cover gradually disappearing as the poor people around us gleaned firewood, the struggle for survival also affected the vervet monkeys. I wrote:

"August 1992, – our monkeys are becoming more aggressive ...yesterday the big male was sitting defiantly on the paw paw tree outside the back door, refusing to move when I tried to pick a fruit! Last week, two others perched up in our mulberry tree urinated on me as I approached to pick some berries to make a pie."

"September, A new big male monkey arrived in our garden at sunrise today. He is chasing and frightening the whole troupe, creating chaos. Baby monkeys are dropping down like falling apples from the very high trees. Our troupe is now retreating from him, with the mothers rapidly descending to the ground to pick up their babies and carry them off, and one little one jumping along on his own to a cassia tree. Our garden males have not yet been able to muster an attack against this invader, as he defiantly eats our fruit, so far there is just retreat and a lot of very noisy agitation."

"October, Last week our two dogs co-operated in a vicious fight to kill our dominant male monkey as he came down to attack them on the ground beside our bamboo clump. I think the dogs must previously have hurt a little monkey, this is why this belligerent male descended on them. Peter says monkeys are terrible fighters and could easily have killed a dog...after all this, the troupe has become cautious, staying safely up in the trees all day, so our strawberries, tomatoes, cabbages, and maize are all having a chance to grow here again."

In our last year the monkey numbers declined to only a vulnerable four. In March 1994 – "I found the remaining big male monkey lying dead in our courtyard, outside the front door today, at teatime. He had obviously gone to that protected spot to die, stretched out on the paving stones between the low wall and a tree trunk. As he had been behaving strangely for two weeks, we suspect he had rabies. He had been fighting a lot in the garden, shrieking, and also sitting on our drawing room window ledge, looking in at us after lunch."

The variety of wild life in our garden was always fascinating. A little water bath attracted many exotic birds, noisy red and green louries, shrikes, darting bulbuls, a jewel like pygmy kingfisher which dived like a stone dropping into the water; majestic crested hoopoes walked across the grass, and brilliant golden orioles perched on branches.

In our last year a covey of wild guinea fowl suddenly migrated to our woods, elegantly flying down to the termite mounds on the lawn, where they contended for these insects with our few remaining monkeys. At dusk, different birds were active, as goshawks swooped to pick up snakes, and a covey of eight trumpeter hornbills calling like geese, would proceed from one tree to another, gleaning fruits.

However, the sovereign creatures of our abode were the long eared African owls, somnolent on a branch outside the kitchen door by day, but powerfully hunting snakes and lizards in the darkness. At night their gentle two-who mating calls mingled with the cries of the bush babies. According to a Chewa proverb 'if an owl sings on the roof at night, then something terrible will happen.'

My diary also recorded insects – "today ants carried a little silver dead snake across our drawing room carpet, and out of the front door. It is a remarkable feat of insect co-operation."

However we suffered a horrendous invasion from well organized ants one February night after torrential rain flooded the garden. Millions amd millions of driver army ants were advancing in formation into the back of our house, crawling under the doors, up the walls and into our windows. It was terrifying, and tired though he was after an emergency call, Michael had to get up to help me kill thousands with boiling water and insecticide. Next morning Peter rebuked me "Madam, you should just have thrown a piece of meat out on the lawn to divert the ants and kill them there. It would have been much easier!"

Walking across our bedroom in socks one evening, I stepped on a little scorpion beside the dressing table, which stung my underfoot. It was very painful for several days.

Writing letters home took much of our time in the evening, such as this one, mentioning events in Mwanza district:

"Dad has just had an interesting patient brought to our hospital from Mwanza after lightning struck and collapsed a witch doctor's house killing several people sheltering there from the thunderstorm. A baby, was on his mother's back when she was killed; so he was brought all the way to our hospital with a ruptured diaphragm – a rare condition. Dad operated successfully to repair the diaphragm.

But now it seems this boy cannot possibly return to his father at Mwanza for a strange reason. His mother's death by the lightning strike proves that she was possessed of an evil spirit like a witch. So by the rules of sorcery, the child's father would have to kill this boy, who must also inherit his mother's bewitchment by this strange injury and death."

And I wrote to my mother in England: "Yesterday I thought I must have cholera, and so did Michael. However after he had seen all the thin and collapsing cholera patients in Mwanza hospital yesterday, he felt more hopeful about me, and today I am better.

I hope you are not worrying about your roof. Did you know that our roof here has leaked badly for nine years, but this year, suddenly, when the rains are heavier than ever before, no water has come in. It is extraordinary because we have done nothing to repair it. I have got used to water dripping in the house, now no more. – Elspeth"

Perhaps my happiest official correspondence was with Queen Elizabeth the Queen Mother through her Ladies in Waiting; she retained her enthusiastic interest in the hospital, encouraging expatriate ladies to help our blood transfusion service, with support from Round Table in Scotland's Blantyre. One of her relatives, Connie Bowes Lyon, was a colonial settler in Malawi, living in a lovely house at the foot of Michiru mountain where she invited us to dinner, telling us about the first Scots pioneers.

Here we saw an old photograph of a sturdy woman in a wide hat climbing Mulanje mountain in 1900. She was a Polish lady who set out from Cape Town, with servants, to walk to Cairo. As she passed through Mulanje, the British district commissioner fell for her. He must have been a rather desperate bachelor, marooned there alone, because the caption noted 'although she looked unattractive, he made advances to her!' She was scared by this most unusual event, and retreating back over the Ruo river into Mozambique, she caught malaria, so her servants carried her back in a machila (hammock) to Mulanje hospital to die.

I wrote to our homesick daughters about our own Ruo River experience: "On Saturday Dad paddled down the Ruo River flowing off Mulanje mountain with a Dutch doctor. I went to the Luchenya River confluence, where an illegal ferry was taking people across to Mozambique from a hidden corner of a tea estate. The ferryman invited me out in his boat to meet Dad, so I made an illegal crossing to Mozambique before going upstream. He said I must not go for a walk over the opposite bank because there is fighting 'pugilistio' every day up there.

This event has had a sequel. At teatime today, a medical assistant from Vila Coutinho hospital in Mozambique suddenly arrived at our home in Blantyre to ask whether we could visit his hospitals over the Mulanje border. They have only medical assistants and no doctors. He spoke good English and said they have no petrol, no drugs, and no medical supplies, but so many hospital patients with very serious injuries. Sadly it would be impossible for us to go."

Musical visitors to our home were of course always a pleasure in deprived and difficult times. When the Berlin RIAS orchestra visited Blantyre, the forty young musicians spent the afternoon at our house, watching our monkeys fighting over the guavas in the garden. The lenghthening shadows of the sunset were made enchanting by their two flautists playing from my book of Mozart duets in the drawing room. This orchestra seemed to belong to the eighteenth century, with the wealth and culture of the rich resounding in the midst of the poverty and illiteracy of Africa; our huge house and lawn became like a classical mansion.

During the difficulties of our later years in Blantyre, some of our happiest evenings were musical ones. We had a surgeons' orchestra with Michael and a Dutch surgeon playing violins, myself as violist, with an American mission surgeon from Thyolo on the harpisichord, his wife as a flautist, and a Dutch veterinary surgeon on the cello. Our drawing room had plenty of space for an orchestra. Harpsichord and flute concertos by Mozart were a solace to these musicians, who were working daily in the tragic situation of malnutrition and disease.

Sipping our coffee, we would hear much about the problems of Thyolo, an area of tea estates up in the Shire highlands, forty miles south of Blantyre. They said the minimum wage for tea pickers on the Thyolo estates had been doubled to the equivalent of just forty pence per day. Rich countries are wealthy because they pay poor countries far too little for their goods, and this unequal trade balance is a major cause of poverty and starvation in Africa.

Then Michael produced another Thyolo tale; he had done an operation at the district hospital, removing the lymph nodes from the groin of a man with penile cancer, to prevent the spread of this malignancy. The patient had already fathered three children. This man surprisingly had undescended testes, positioned in the groin, which is usually said to cause infertility because the higher temperature inside the body discourages spermatogenesis.

Another doctor noted how AIDS was changing family life and mentioned the new situation of grandmas, with anecdotes which may replace standard concepts about old age:

"Today I saw again a grandma who last came to me two years ago, bringing her daughter and son in law, both dying of AIDS. They left behind seven orphans to go into her care. As this penniless grandma could not buy enough food for eight mouths, she had to join the prostitutes in Thyolo. Now she too has become infected with HIV and is dying.

So these seven orphans will have to go to the great-grandmother. Will this great grandma who is tiny, frail, and very poor, endure the same cruel fate?" This belies the dogma 'people beget many children as an insurance for their old age'. And it also challenges the traditional picture of a grandma in folk stories like Red Riding Hood. The disease AIDS produces a family situation like Grimm's fairy tales going in reverse gear.

A little more light heartedly we heard another Thyolo medical tale – an order of nuns had sent one of their novices to hospital because of her persistent symptoms. She swore she was a virgin but her HIV-test was positive. Was this a case of the 'immaculate infection'?

The vet told us rabies was becoming a far more dangerous disease in the impoverishment of crowded Malawi. The rabies virus is passed in the saliva of an infected animal. Two years ago his clinic had reduced rabies in Blantyre dogs to two cases per month, by vaccinnation campaigns. Now, the Malawi government had run out of money to buy this expensive vaccine and he was seeing several rabid dogs each week again.

All doctors describe rabies as one of the most terrible ways to die. It is a disease that can be prevented but not cured. The incubation period lasts from three months to one year. Spasms of the oesophagus develop, and an old treatment recommended chloroform inhalations. A British girl at our school died of rabies three months after being nipped by a small puppy. The whole school was then innoculated with fourteen injections of vaccine in the abdomen, which was the only treatment available in 1976.

Without dog vaccine in Malawi after 1989, rabies spread. By 1993 five patients died of rabies at one district hospital in two weeks. When people arrived complaining of being bitten by rabid dogs, there was no prophylactic vaccine to prevent the onset of this, among the worst of all diseases. And by 1996, twenty three victims died in Lilongwe in a month.

Other medical visitors coming to dinner talked about the return of another serious disease in the nineties, Sleeping Sickness. This was also due to increased population pressure on the available land. A physician mentioned three comatose soldiers lying in Mangochi hospital, all with swollen neck glands and said to be infected with HIV. But her diagnosis was sleeping sickness, transmitted into human blood by a tsetse fly. The elongated trypanosomes thrive in the blood plasma for months, until they finally invade the solid internal organs and the brain in the terminal stages. If treated very early, Sleeping Sickness can be cured with drugs.

This sleeping sickness parasite is spread to humans by tsetse flies from its reservoir in wild antelopes like nyala, kudu, and buck, in bush areas at a certain altitude. Impala have a special physiological 'shivering' mechanism which prevents tsetse flies biting them. As more and more landless Malawians were looking for gardens to cultivate in the nineties, they moved up hill into the tsetse fly belt around Nkhota Kota game reserve, resulting in many sleeping sickness deaths in that district. The park warden told us his wife had just died of it. One successful foreign aid project organized simple baited tsetse fly traps in the tsetse belt areas of Malawi.

Life had other aspects though. We always enjoyed journeys through the wild, mountainous landscape. Once, stopping by a meadow, I picked a bouquet of grasses in lush seed, yellow daisies, mint, and rosemary. The eagles were calling from the steep crags, larks were singing, and flocks of swifts were darting for insects over the long grass. A brilliant sunset then cast crimson light over the soaring, granite, mountain peaks. I was always sad to leave Africa, even for a short time.

However, we could not stay young and robust enough to work in a huge hospital for ever, and a fascinating era of our lives was coming to an end.

After eighteen happy years, we decided to leave Blantyre in November 1994, sadly realising that a struggle for survival would come with the rapidly increasing human population around this old city. My diary recorded some of the difficulties of our last months in Blantyre:

"Tuesday – Michael now has bad problems in the hospital. The laundry has broken down and there is a shortage of linen for operating. Two patients urgently needing laparotomy last night, who had been brought as serious emergencies from a hundred miles away, had to be left until today. The hospital has run out of pethidine and morphia for post-operative pain. He has to fight for any linen with obstetrics and try to persuade them to do half as many caesars today."

"Wednesday – First I transported a villager dying of AIDS to the hospital, but the pharmacy has run out of drugs to help him. Then, on my way to a ladies' tea party, I saw a terrible sight that is happening in many districts, with the new mob justice since democratic elections – a crowd was taking the law into its own hands and burning an alleged thief alive in Chitawira township. I dared not stop, because our cook had warned me it would be dangerous. So on I sped, and from roasting thieves alive, I was suddenly launched into a hen party at a pseudo-Tudor house. It was perhaps more of a shock to step into the insulated world of the rich than to live amongst the struggle for survival by the poor.

When I came home at dusk, Michael was summoned to a patient who had been stabbed in the heart with a screw driver wielded by a thief as he walked along the street."

Within three months of our departure from the South to North Malawi, most of the fine, ancient trees, planted a century ago by British colonial pioneers to form the woods around our beloved home, had been felled to sell as firewood – dozens of pine trees and giant blue gums, and so many more blossoming trees – red Flames of the Forest, mauve Jacarandas, white Bauhinias, a towering African Tulip Tree, scented Frangipannis, Oleanders, Poinsettias, Locust Beans, yellow Cassias, and also a host of fruit trees – Mangoes, Avocados, Mulberrys, Guavas, Loquats, Bananas, and Peaches. So we moved on to our wilder semi-retirement home beside Lake Malawi, still to serve the district hospitals.

Chapter 17. Health for All MK

Was it only failure to face reality in 1978 that allowed the World Health Organization to declare "Health for All by the Year 2000"? Or was there a compromising desire for comfortable words to mask uncomfortable facts? 'Community Health' was to be achieved by primary health care, maternal and child health, food security, clean water, and more recently AIDS awareness and family planning. This is still a powerful lobby and places emphasis on preventive measures. It should operate through health policies, and village health workers visiting rural and urban areas, giving talks and demonstrations, encouraging participation in building improved latrines or protected wells and so on. These are admirable ideas but require adequate funding to have any effect, since it is expensive on professional time and transport.

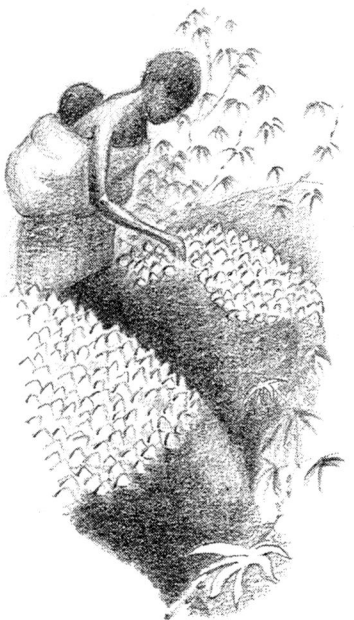

This scheme is probably workable in rich countries but has not had much success in poor African nations. In two decades of its operation in Malawi, disease incidence has increased and maternal and child mortality have not improved. This is not surprising since the main needs of many communities are food and increasingly, water - not clean water, just any water. The underlying problems are the related ones of poverty and over-population. It is worth reflecting that if community health schemes were successful, the population would be even greater and less sustainable.

Increasing numbers of sick crowd the crumbling structures of the curative services in poor countries begging for help. Health budgets in real terms are declining. There are few medical staff yet 'Community Health' lobbies for funds to be used and efforts to be diverted to chase after an unresponsive 'well' public. Solutions to community welfare problems will not come from the medical field, but but from the more significant economic, and business sector.

Mother drying cassava flour on rocks

Too much is expected of medicine and health care, and more humility is required. The World Bank, World Health Organization, UNICEF, and other Aid agencies promote Community Health, but are less willing to support hospital resources. Hospitals set up in the colonial era are and have become a part of the structure of the community, but are now under great strain.

The more one sees of these UN agencies, and bodies such as the European Union, the more they are in danger of becoming grandiose clubs, with the members unwilling to step out of line for fear of jeopardizing their life style. A greatly scaled down and more efficient co-ordinating world body in health is needed. Rich countries would do well to reconsider the scale of their contributions and use the money saved for their own aid schemes, which are usually better supervised and more accountable.

'Per Diem' payments to workshop attenders can be an example of misuse of funds, often producing a negative impact on health. I once visited a district hospital in which three of the five clinical officers were away on various workshops organized by UN agencies on 'AIDS Awareness, MCH, and the Health Media'. The per diem allowances for a four day workshop might equal a clinical officer's monthly salary.

The participants are of course pleased to attend but they have often told me that little new was discussed, or sometimes obvious or unworkable ideas are put forward. Donors promote workshops since they are an acceptable and easy way of off-loading their funds. However little 'work' gets done, and what is sold is often of little value. No heads of state turned up at the recent (1999) conference on AIDS in Lusaka; one of the several reasons could be that they realized that little will be achieved by talking about it.

I was once sent as the Malawian representative to a surgical staffing workshop funded by the WHO in Nairobi. In three days my per diems amounted to more than I could spend. At the airport, since Kenyan shillings could not be exchanged, I bought a coral necklace for Elspeth with the ill gotten gains. I hope the tax payers of the rich world will forgive this small expense, but they should not forgive the lavish spending by UN agencies.

There is now a 'per diem' mentality in the poor world. For example, when a mission hospital, which monitors its funds carefully, wants to set up a community participation scheme for improving water supply or child nutrition, one of the first questions put by the villagers who will benefit from this scheme is 'how much is the per diem'? If it is not enough then few will turn up.

Places on the well funded AIDS workshops are often commandeered by the influential non-clinical staff of a hospital or ministry, and there is a wry joke about some people getting fat on AIDS, not slim.

Negative impacts occur in other unexpected, sad ways in international aided community health projects. The placing of expatriate volunteers can often be a problem in a poor country. In health schemes they are commonly single women out of college posted to a district hospital to work on MCH, AIDS Awareness, breast feeding or child survival. The district health officer will have to find, with difficulty, accommodation and a Malawian co-worker/translator. He will often protest in vain that he does not want them but the aid agencies will persist. The local Malawians do not respect a white female talking to them, through an interpreter, about intimate and cultural matters. However when trained volunteers offer technical skills in engineering, education, and business projects, they can contribute a great deal.

Participation by the community is an essential part of community health, indeed until people actually want to change, no change is possible. Unfortunately the really vulnerable groups often fail to get involved because of their poverty. They may become increasingly dependent on 'handouts' and free food schemes.

A chilling way out of this sort of dependency comes from West Africa. A region participated in a 'revolving drug scheme'. Sufficient essential drugs (anti-malarials and antibiotics) to last a year were supplied free. The donor and the elders discussed charges to be made, so that by the end of the year there would be enough funds to purchase next year's supply, and so on. The compassionate elders failed to agree to the donor's price guides and prices were set too low. The next year fewer drugs could be purchased. When they ran out of stock, the donor was approached and told 'our people are dying', but the scheme had finished. The community then met and decided to set aside a certain percentage of their crops and wages towards the drug fund. The scheme was thus established on a sustainable basis.

In Malawi such a cost recovery charging scheme for health services was proposed in the early 1990s but never implemented due to political timidity and infighting. So the health service deterioration continues. Regular large donations of drugs, equipment, and vehicles, keep it from collapsing. We ourselves help in a small way on our surgical visits since all our air baggage allowance plus extra is taken up by sutures, catheters, drugs, and medical equipment. Some of it is purchased with donations and some discarded from UK hospitals.

Broken vehicles outside hospital

In the district hospitals I visit, over 80% of the major surgery is on women. All is maternal related, Caesarian sections, ruptured uterus, ectopic pregnancy, and 'evacuation' after abortions. The numbers increase every year, and mens' needs are crowded out in order to conserve scarce sutures, drugs, and staff time for these emergencies. Almost all these operations are done not by doctors, but by the clinical officers. Even well into the next millenium it will be the affordable, good clinical cfficers who will contine to do most of the surgery in Malawi.

The increasing birthrate puts great stress on the country, the countryside, and the hospital services, as does the number of backstreet abortions. Before the AIDS epidemic it was the major cause of admission in young females and a major cause of death and disability. If a girl survives in the village, she may need to be admitted for scraping out (evacuation) of any remains; if not she may develop peritonitis or worse, as in this daughter of a civil servant (who would be expelled from school if she was pregnant):

She was sixteen years old and had eighteen inches of large bowel hanging out from her bottom. The stick used for her abortion had penetrated the uterus and hooked on to the bowel and pulled it out. At operation, after tidying up and removing dead intestines, a colostomy was made. Two months later, after she had recovered and gained weight at home, this was closed and the continuity of the colon restored, allowing normal bowel action. She was very lucky although almost certainly now unable to bear children.

Before the introduction of modern contraception, village abortion was the commonest form of birth control in much of the poor world. When modern contraception was introduced (the Pill, the coil, and the depoprovera injection), it was not part of the packages offered to the poorest women in the world because of the Vatican veto in the United Nations. We lost the opportunity to save millions from mutilating backstreet abortions, and lessen the degradation of the earth. 'Family Planning for All by the Year 2000' now that would have been a worthwhile and probably achievable declaration.

Contraception and family planning advice is today part of most health aid schemes although it seems to work best as a separate 'dedicated' project and not integrated into primary health. Even so it fails to reach many in need with regular supplies. Especially in need are HIV-positive mothers, and a third of pregnant women in Malawi carry this virus. A further pregnancy will accelerate the course of the final AIDS related illness causing the woman's early death, and then orphaning her other children. Any baby born to this mother is likely to die within two years, indeed it is now one of the main causes of infant death.

In the rich world, pregnant mothers infected with HIV are advised and offered a termination of pregnancy. This was recommended at a meeting of all the Professional Medical Associations of SubSaharan African countries in Blantyre in March 1992. But this resolution has not been implemented in most countries with major HIV epidemics. Is it because the law makers are men? Only in Zambia and South Africa is safe medical abortion legal.

Abortion is an unpleasant subject, shocking and disquieting, but it will not go away and must be faced if there is to be health for many young women. If it were legalized it would place an increasing burden on the overworked health services, but the reduction in the major problems occurring with unsafe abortion would offset this to some extent, and it could pay its way. In rich countries termination is offered in the case of failure of contraception. There are 'morning after' and medical contraception pills that are being introduced in Malawi. This will be of great benefit to desperate women.

Finally, if Health for All is to be more than an empty comfortable slogan, population policies must play a large part. Today in Malawi, and much of the world, malnutrition, illiteracy and unemployment are increasing, income and food production per head are decreasing. The acceptable, safe, response to population growth from international aid is to talk about female empowerment and education and poverty alleviation, it is said that 'if people see their children live, they will have fewer'.

Many of these approaches have yet to be seen to work in Africa (as compared to Asia) and in any case will take too long. Increasing poverty, hunger, and strife will come first. China is one of the few countries that has faced up to the issue. In most of Africa there has been no determined political will to consider this problem. Fragile democracies are wary of it; coalition politics and cross party agreements are needed. Previous autocrats including Hastings Banda denied there was a problem, and beware anyone who disagreed with him. Headmen and politicians with several wives and many children can hardly take up this issue with conviction.

As expatriates who have lived most of our life in the poor world, and seeing the Aid givers unthinkingly making this situation worse, it is difficult to keep silent on the issue. It is of course easy to have an opinion, but some countries, including Malawi, are becoming increasingly 'un-self-sustainable' due to a treatable cause. As a doctor, I believe that if there is a cure for an ill it should be offered. If it is refused, and self harm continues, either you shrug your shoulders or firmer action has to be taken for the sake of the patient or the community.

Poor countries are increasingly dependent on rich nations and it would be unethical for the wealthy to shrug their shoulders, but this is the trend as aid fatigue sets in. If less aid is becoming available, at least it should be spent wisely, on supporting existing services for example, and relieving the debt burden. Forget about development; this may follow from within the country and its entrepreneurs who deserve every support. Unless income generation is indigenous it is likely to fail, and there are many examples of this throughout Africa and in Malawi.

Donors have imposed democratic conditionality on aid, help is only given if there is transparency and free elections. Has the time come for some sort of demographic conditionality? If Aid is short, it should be given to those communities which are shown to face their problems of malnutrition, soil degradation, and deforestation square on; for example those which increased their contraceptive uptake and decreased their birthrate. Furthermore the two child or one child family could be encouraged by tax cuts, or other incentives. Instead of free maize being given to pregnant mothers (as happened in 1994, encouraging more pregnancies) it could be given to those having tubal ligation or a vasectomy to help them over the healing period. There could be assistance with school books and uniforms for only two children in the family.

When these views are discussed with donors and recipients they regard this as part and parcel of a naive attitude and look grim. We will all be more grim in the future when facing famine or strife. For what humanitarian answer other than population restriction is possible?

Improving crop yields? - Genetically manipulated crops usually need fertilizer and irrigation if they are to succeed. There is little suitable land left, fertilizer is imported and expensive. Fair prices from the rich world for cash crops would help.

Emigration? - To where? This will probably store up future conflict.
The flood of people from poor countries is likely to lead to a 'fortress mentality' in rich nations.

Industrialization? - Unlikely to happen; even the indigenous textile industry is swamped by the second hand clothes market and goods from the industrialized countries will be cheaper.

Increasing employment? - How? The unemployed youth numbers grow every day. Local business and investment should certainly be given every encouragement.

What other than population restraint is possible for the poor, by the poor, to allow them the dignity of more control over their destiny?

If we fail to face the issues 'we deceive ourselves and the truth is not in us' as the Book of Common Prayer has it. Indeed there is need for prayer, or something very like it, and responding resolutions if the health of the poor and the planet is not to continue its decline. So what resolutions? How can we improve, recover, even compensate our earth, and make amends. What about Amendment Aid?

Chapter 18.   Amendment

In our thirty fascinating years in Central and Southern Africa, we have sadly witnessed a declining quality of life for the majority of inhabitants. On the other hand, wealthy countries are experiencing increasing pollution, traffic congestion, mega-cities, and loss of green fields to 'development'. These nations comprise 20% of mankind and utilize 80% of the world's resources.

We, rich and poor, are spoiling our mother earth. A unique species of plant or animal is lost every day, due to habitat destruction. Development has become a dirty word.

If we cannot reverse the trend we must at least make amends. The rich should not let profit motives govern their actions but have a global, responsible conscience. This will include responsible Aid, Development Aid?, Amendment Aid?, to the poor.

It is younger, enlightened Africans who, through church, professional and business lobbies, will face the problem of unsustainable population growth and effect the necessary cultural reformation.

The rich should learn the lessons of the past decades and refrain from imposing solutions. However, continuing technical assistance is needed in maintaining public services such as roads, communications, agriculture, hospitals, and family planning.

Less privileged nations can preserve and share some aspects of their heritage. In the case of Malawi, close to our hearts, these are the natural beauty of the land, the warmth of the people, and the fruits of their labours.

In these ways we may narrow the Great Rift between us and begin the healing of our planet, safeguarding our grandchildrens' inheritance.

156 Amendment Aid

Lake Path

Appendix Brief History of Malawi

The original inhabitants were hunter gatherer bushmen, who left red geometric paintings in several caves. Around 1300 A.D. the Bantu tribal migrations were spreading southwards from the Congo.

In the early nineteenth century, the Yao tribes came in from Mozambique in the east, sailing across Lake Nyasa in Arab dhows and settling around the southern lakeshore. This was the time of the slave trade; in some years as many as thirty thousand Africans were taken across the Lake to go to the Mozambique coast. Then the Ngoni, a warlike, male dominated, Zulu tribe also migrated from Natal to northern Nyasaland in the 1830s, fighting many battles with the local people.

It was into these many conflicts that David Livingstone's Zambesi Expedition reached the Shire River and Lake Nyasa in 1859. The early Christian missionaries established schools, hospitals, and agricultural and commercial projects, that became the basis of Nyasaland's peace and progress. In 1889, Nyasaland became a British Protectorate under Queen Victoria, in whose name gunboats were sent to attack Arab slave dhows on the Lake. British colonial rule was effective for sixty years. The colony became part of the Federation of Rhodesia and Nyasaland for eleven years 1953-64, and the independent state of Malawi was established in 1964.

Statistics

Malawi is a land about the size of England with scant natural resources. Her people rely mainly on subsistence agriculture to produce their daily food of maize, cassava, and vegetables. Tea, coffee, sugar cane, cotton, and tobacco, are grown as cash crops.

The annual 3.3% rate of population increase is predicted to drop to 2.2% annually with the AIDS epidemic. Malawi's population is expected to double in size in the next twenty years. The average fertility rate is 7.6 children per woman, with life expectancy of forty one years. The child mortality rate is 324 per 1,000.

About half the population is under fifteen years. The economically active labour force increases by 145,000 job seekers each year, for only 15,000 job vacancies. The most striking trend in the past decade had been the drop in real wages and incomes. Malawi's debt owed to World Bank and the IMF is £1,401 million. Each Malawian carries a an annual burden of £140 of this external debt, which is more than the £109 the average Malawian can hope to earn in an entire year. Foreign aid forms 40% of government expenditure

Tree felling has caused forest cover to halve in thirty years.

72% of Malawian subsistence farmers now work smallholdings of less than 1.0 hectare, considered to be the smallest garden size required to attain bare minimum food for a household of five people. A quarter of households cultivate less than half a hectare.

Population of Nyasaland – Malawi

Year	Population	Year	Population
1900	800,000	1970	5,000,000
1930	1,500,000	1980	7,500,000
1950	2,000,000	1990	10,000,000

Bibliography – Further Reading

"The Narrative for an Expedition to the Zambesi and its Tributaries" David Livingstone (John Murray 1865).

"Nyassa, a Journal of Adventures" by E.D.Young R.N., London, 1877.

"The Story of my Life" Harry Johnston, London, Chatto and Windus 1923.

"Averting a world food shortage: tighten your belts for Cairo II" Maurice King and Charles Elliott, British Medical Journal, 1996, Volume 313, 995-7.

Dallabeta G.A. et al. "High Socio-economic status as a risk factor for HIV-infection but not for Sexually Transmitted Diseases in Women in Malawi: Implication for HIV-1 control." Journal of Infectious Diseases 1993; 167: 36-42.

World Bank AIDS Assessment Study, Malawi 1997.

Situation Analysis of Poverty in Malawi, United Nations and the Government of Malawi, 1993.

"Where Silence Rules – The Suppression of Dissent in Malawi" Richard Carver, 1990, Human Rights Watch.

"Malawi, Wildlife, Parks and Reserve" Judy Carter, Macmillan, London, 1987.

"On the Fever of East Central Africa encountered by Livingstone's Zambesi Expedition" by Charles J. Meller The Lancet for October 22nd and November 5th 1864.

"Laws of Livingstonia" W. P. Livingstone, Hodder and Stoughton, London, 1921.

"Zambesi Journal and Letters 1858-63" Sir John Kirk, Oliver and Boyd, Edinburgh 1934.

"The Situation of Children and Women in Malawi" UNICEF, Lilongwe 1987.

"Days gone by" Bishop J. E. Hine, John Murray, London 1924.

"Travels and Researches among the Lakes and Mountains of East and Central Africa" J. F. Elton, John Murray, London 1879.

"The Zambesi Journal of James Stewart 1862-1863" edited by J. P. R. Wallis, Chatto and Windus, London 1952.

"The Story of Medicine and Disease in Malawi – The 130 Years since Livingstone" Michael and Elspeth King, 1992, third impression 1997.

Further copies of 'The Great Rift' and 'The Story of Medicine and Disease in Malawi' available from
DAUNT BOOKS
83 Marylebone High St., London W1M 3DE

Tel: 020-7224 2295 Fax: 020-7224 6893
Email: orders@dauntbooks.com